W9-ADH-209

Teaching Children to Become INDEPENDENT READERS

Teaching Children to Become INDEPENDENT READERS

Margaret LaPray

THE CENTER FOR APPLIED RESEARCH IN EDUCATION, INC.
521 Fifth Avenue, New York, N.Y. 10017

THE CENTER FOR APPLIED
RESEARCH IN EDUCATION, INC.
New York

Library of Congress
Catalog Card Number: 74-174465

Printed in the United States of America

C-8662-3

DEDICATION

À mes trois soeurs, Ardyce, Edith, et Marie, qui m'ont aidée, encouragée, et inspirée. (Which freely translated means—to my three sisters, who aided, edited, and abetted me.)

ABOUT THE AUTHOR

Dr. Margaret LaPray received a Master of Arts degree from the University of Minnesota and a Doctor of Philosophy degree from Cornell University. She became a member of the San Diego State College faculty in 1957. At present, she is Professor of Education and Director of Learning Difficulties at the San Diego State College Clinical Training Center.

Dr. LaPray teaches advanced courses in reading, conducts annual research projects, and is a frequent contributor to professional journals. She is co-author, with Dr. Ramon Ross, of the primary readers in the new Lyons and Carnahan Young American Basal Readers.

ABOUT THIS BOOK

This book is designed as a ready reference in reading instruction. It gives the teacher informal inventories, which can serve as tools for assessing each child's present performance and planning success-oriented lessons based on *what he knows*. The book also provides numerous games, activities, and interest-builders which will stimulate and motivate children toward more effectual reading experiences.

Initially the activities concentrate on successful first steps in reading, since the child's tolerance of failure during this early period is minimal. Emphasis is given first to familiarizing the child with the shape and location of letters in word forms. The child is provided opportunities to recognize these components of reading through pleasant experiences and association in much the same way that he becomes familiar with notes, staffs, and the joy of singing before he is expected to read from a musical score.

Basically, the philosophy of the author is that, given an opportunity, every physically normal child can learn to read, whether he is intellectually average, gifted, or a slow learner. First, the child needs to discover that it is more profitable *to read* than to *not read*. Next, daily diagnosis enables the teacher to build on what is known and to focus on teaching what is missing. By becoming sensitive to the child's rate and pattern of learning, the teacher can teach in ways that are economical of hers and the child's time.

A basic premise in this book is that the focal point of the reading program is the student and his particular pattern of learning. The author strongly feels that a student in the process of acquiring word-attack skills has totally different needs from students who have already acquired these skills; consequently, an "individualized reading program" that is appropriate for those who have already acquired some of these skills is inappropriate for those who have none. At the other extreme, it is equally inappropriate to slavishly follow a basic reading program, teaching digraphs, phonograms, and affixes, with students who already read fifth-grade level and beyond with *no* vocabulary difficulty. The emphasis throughout the chapters is on discovering the child's style of learning and tailoring the reading program to fit it.

Vocabulary and concepts found in content fields are related to the child's own experiences. Reciprocal questioning is described since it involves the child in learning skills that lead to independence in reading. Follow-through activities become the responsibility of the child. The child selects whatever skill he needs to have strengthened and designs an exercise to teach this skill.

This book is intended to be thoroughly practical. While the content is directed toward elementary school teachers, ideas are usable at the secondary level by teachers working with nonreaders or retarded readers.

Margaret LaPray

Table of Contents

PART III: PLACING A VALUE ON READING

Appendices

Content *Page*

Teaching Children to Become
INDEPENDENT READERS

PART I

MAKING DAILY DIAGNOSIS A REALITY

1

REACTING SUCCESSFULLY TO READING

A number of roads lead to the development of a good reader. However, some roads are devious, some are filled with potholes, detours, and even dead-ends. Our aim is to avoid these time-consuming delays which can so often be disastrous. While a direct road is feasible for most children, for others a winding, scenic route may produce greater interest as well as higher reading achievement.

Words act as the catalyst that turns Cinderella into a princess, a frog into a prince, and ennui into excitement. Poverty-stricken is the native speaker of English who has not yet learned to associate the language he speaks and the experience he understands word-for-word in print. This book is dedicated to the premise that all people are created *unequal* and that reading is an equalizer of limitless potential.

All children react to reading. The mandate of the teacher is to be so sensitive to the child's attitude toward, and curiosity about reading, that these two prognosticators of future achievement can be assessed through direct observation of the child's behavior, or indirectly through paper-and-pencil measures, such as *An Inventory of Reading Attitude* and the *Individual Reading Attitude Assessment*, which can be found in Appendix II. These indirect measures are appropriate for the child who has already begun to read.

The child who reacts negatively toward reading as a result of what he perceives to be too much pressure could be helped through parent-teacher conferences, child-teacher discussions, and children's "rap" groups. Such a child discovers that the world still revolves whether he reads "x" number of books or not. Another child, blasé and disinterested in mundane stories, can be shown books dealing with real problems such as, *Egypt Game*[1] or *The Sugar Pear Tree.*[2] If several students in the class are unenthusiastic about reading, the program needs instant change to include such things as Book Fairs, Book Clubs, U.S.S.R. (Uninterrupted Sustained Silent Reading),[3] Book Swaps, or whatever else it takes to invigorate the reading climate.

TEACHERS ON THIN ICE

Excessive pressure and drab content are not the only reasons for a child reacting negatively toward reading. There are many other causes. In the beginning he may have been treated as a skilled reader, when in fact he had not yet developed word-attack skills. A pitfall to avoid is total acceptance of the opinions of the so-called experts (often specialists without experience in teaching *beginning* reading), who recognize no difference between a beginning reader and a reader who has learned to apply word-attack skills. To assume that a beginning reader can respond like a skilled reader is as preposterous as to assume that a beginning skater can perform like a skilled skater. Just as the beginning skater must learn the basics of maintaining balance, controlling wobbly ankles, and putting one foot ahead of the other, so too, the beginning reader has some basic steps to learn. Occasionally, a child is termed a natural skater just as he may be termed a natural reader. In both of these cases, the child learns so effortlessly that the usual basic sequence of learning has been internalized, and it appears to the observer that these steps have been skipped. These unusual cases will be easy to identify through tests which inventory their skills. The majority of children, however, do not fall into this special category, and they will need varying degrees of specific instruction.

---

[1] Zilpha Snyder, *Egypt Game* (New York: Atheneum, 1967).

[2] Clyde Bulla, *The Sugar Pear Tree* (New York: Crowell, 1960).

[3] Lyman, Hunt Jr., "The Effect of Self-Selection, Interest, and Motivation upon Independent, Instructional, and Frustrational Levels," *The Reading Teacher,* 24, No. 2 (Nov. 1970), 146-151.

WORDS AS BASIC UNITS

As soon as the child recognizes his name in graphic form, he can be taught to read an action word. A direct command such as "John, jump!" is a sentence and at the same time an action that he can demonstrate. Words are the basic units in reading the English language. The child who memorizes a sentence or page is complimented for having a good memory. If he cannot then identify each word separately, he is not considered to be reading and his parents and teacher are disappointed. They should, however, be pleased that the child has already shown his ability to listen closely, memorize easily, and associate pictures and content. It is an easy step to teach him words by pulling them out of context, writing them separately, and analyzing them. Even though the child learns to read simple sentences, actor-action, (John, jump!) he still must identify any *new* word used with his name.

OVERVIEW OF METHODS AND MATERIALS

Of the limitless methods and materials available, none are infallible nor without some merit. Teachers caught up in the enthusiasms of research claims, testimonials, and innovations find reading a fascinating field. The seemingly miraculous results attributed to the methods and materials in use today are, in a large measure, due to the personality of the reporter. Some examples, together with sources for further description of the methods, follow:

Self-Selection
: Jeannette Veatch, *Individualizing Your Reading Program* (New York: Putnam's, 1959).

Visceral Level Reading
: Sylvia Ashton-Warner, *Teacher* (New York: Simon & Schuster, 1963).

Visual, Auditory, and Kinesthetic Linkage
: Anna Gillingham, *Remedial Training for Children with Specific Disabilities in Reading, Spelling, and Penmanship* (Cambridge, Mass.: Educational Publishing Service, 1960).

Kinesthetic Method
: Grace M. Fernald, *Remedial Techniques in Basic School Subjects* (New York: McGraw-Hill, 1966).

I.T.A. (Initial Teaching Alphabet)
: John Downing, "The I.T.A. (Initial Teaching Alphabet) Reading Experiment," *The Reading Teacher*, 18 (Nov. 1964), 105-110.

Color-Coded Reading
Caleb Gattegno, *Background and Principles: Words in Color* (Chicago: Encyclopedia Britannica, n.d.).
Physical Retraining
Clark Delacato, *New Start for the Child with Reading Problems* (New York: McKay, 1970).
Glenn Doman, *How to Teach Your Baby to Read* (Westminster: Random, 1964).
Talking Typewriter
Omar Kayam Moore, " 'Tis Time He Should Begin to Read," *Carnegie Corporation of New York Quarterly*, Vol. 9 (April 1951), pp. 1-3.
Aural-Oral Reading
Bill Martin, *Sounds of Language Readers*, Teacher's Manuals (New York: Holt, Rinehart & Winston, 1966).
Neurological Impress
R. G. Heckelman, "Using the Neurological Impress Remedial Technique," *Academic Therapy Quarterly*, 1, No. 4 (DeWitt Reading Clinic, 1543 Fifth Avenue, San Rafael, California, n.d.).
Team Reading
Donald Durrell, *Improving Reading Instruction* (Cleveland: World Book Co., 1956).
Programmed Reading
M. W. Sullivan and Cynthia Dee Buchanan, *Programmed Reading* (St. Louis: Webster Division of McGraw-Hill Book Co., 1964).
Sensory Involvement
Maria Montessori, *Montessori Method* (New York: Schocken Books, Inc., 1964).
Language Experience
Roach Van Allen, *Language Experience in Reading* (Chicago: Encyclopedia Britannica, 1966).

The teacher should be aware that a great part of the success in using methods or materials is due to the catalystic quality of the reporter. Each teacher must have a dedication toward the materials and methods best suited to her, while at the same time keeping in mind the needs of her students. From the myriads of methods, teachers make a commitment:

1. To teach *all* children by a particular method:
   a. parts to wholes–(sounds/letters to build words: /kaet/ = cat)
   b. Gestalts (aural-oral, neurological impress)
2. To teach from a variety of methods by the one most economical from the child's viewpoint.

To illustrate this, Economy Press is one of many examples of *Item 1a* in the previous organization, since the method begins with the identification of phonemes/graphemes (sounds/letters; in this instance, vowels) which are later blended into words. One advantage of teaching by such a method is that the slowest child in the class is not likely to fail. A disadvantage is, however, that superior readers will be held back. Consequently, they are less likely to discover the sheer joy of reading and may even develop a distaste for it.

Language experience is one of many approaches which may be classed as *Item 1b* in the previous organization. In contrast to *Item 1a*, language experience penalizes the slow reader and frees the superior reader to progress more rapidly. *Item 2*, which is more difficult to administer, is the most appropriate for all learners since it attempts to match the learner with the approach which is best for him.

From the wealth of materials, teachers make a similar commitment to one of two procedures:

1. They channel *all* children through identical reading materials (all basal, all great books, all programmed readers, or any combination of these).
2. They simultaneously run several channels with differing materials (some basals, some self-selection, some programmed readers, or combinations of these).

The first program is identical for the total class. Each child completes one level of books and proceeds to the next level at different times, but in the exact same sequence. The expectancy is identical for all students in the class. Even linear-programmed readers, such as the Sullivan books, are individualized mainly in the dimension of *time*. Some children may enter the program at different points than others and may proceed through it rapidly, but a few may progress at a snail's pace, if at all.

The second program necessitates surveying the child's interest, experience, and talent and matching materials appropriate to these findings. In many instances, the child can assist in this selection. Obviously, the second type of program is the most difficult to administer, but the most likely to equalize the child's opportunity for success.

The major emphasis in this book is on the second program or simultaneous reading tracks. To implement this program it is necessary to assess what is known and build on this, and also discover what is not known and fill this need. The process of assessing readers begins at the readiness stage, and it is this particular phase that will be discussed in Chapter 1.

In assessing reading readiness, we start with the assumption that to learn to read easily, a child must be able to match letters, know that letters can be written in capital or lower case, and understand that letters make up words in our written language.

CONCEPT OF LETTERS

If we accept the preceding assumption, then we need to assess the child to see whether he already has these skills or whether they need to be taught. The following instrument is designed to serve this purpose. The test can be used with any nonreader of elementary school age who can recognize his name. These test items may be duplicated by the teacher. Have each child mark the seven parts of the following test according to the teacher's oral directions: See Appendix 1, pages 185 and 186 for the Readiness Test format.

READING READINESS TEST

Part I: Letters

Oral Directions

Note to teacher: Each flash card is shown, without naming the letter on it.

1. "Point to the first box at the top of the page with letters of the alphabet in it. Find and circle all of the letters in your first name.

2. Point to the box with a balloon in it. Look at this flash card and see this letter– b . The first word starts with this letter and there is a dotted line around it. Trace over the dotted line with your pencil. Find and circle three other words that begin with this same letter.

Children's Test Sheet

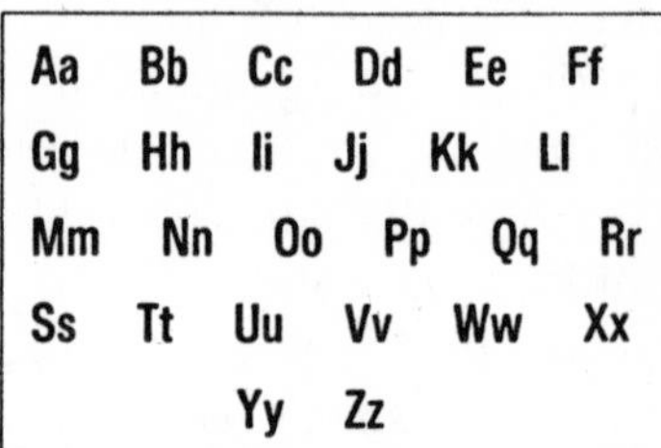

Aa Bb Cc Dd Ee Ff
Gg Hh Ii Jj Kk Ll
Mm Nn Oo Pp Qq Rr
Ss Tt Uu Vv Ww Xx
Yy Zz

Figure 1-1

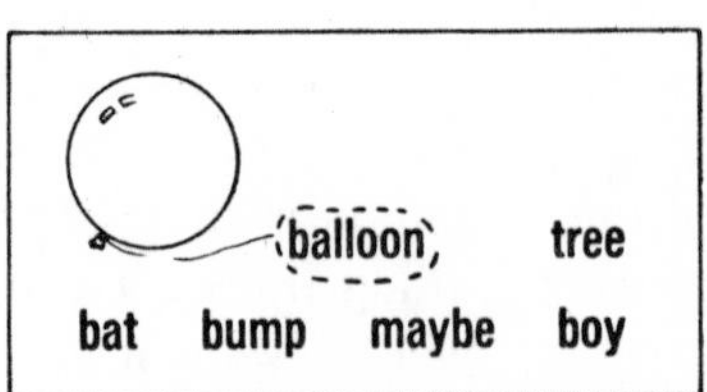

Figure 1-2

3. Point to the box with a bike in it. Look at this letter on the flash card–[k]. Look at the first word. Do you see this letter in the beginning of the word? . . . Is it at the end? . . . Is it in the middle of the word? . . . Look at the next word. Do you see this letter–[k]–in the middle of it? It is circled for you. Trace the dotted lines. Find and circle three other words with this letter in the *middle*.

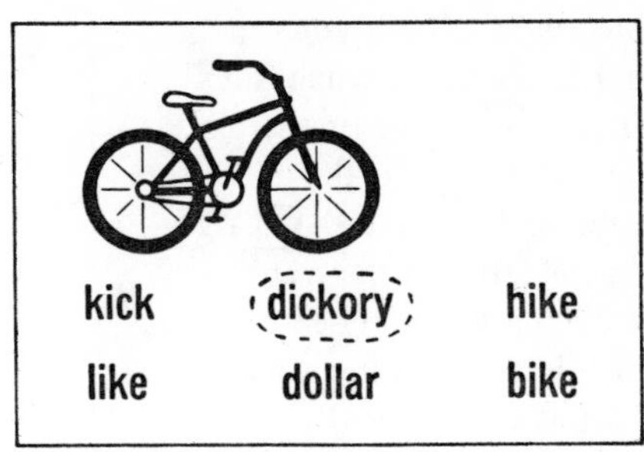

Figure 1-3

4. Point to the box with two baseball bats. Look at this letter–[s]. Look at the first word. Does it have this letter at the end? It is circled for you. Find and circle three other words that end with this letter. Point to the next box.

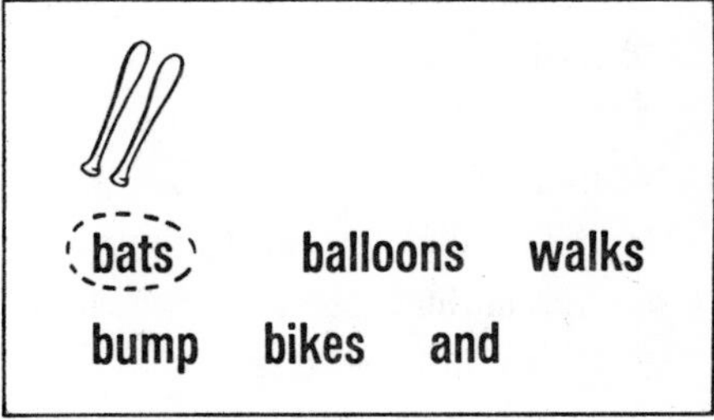

Figure 1-4

5. The word bottle begins with this letter–[b]. Circle the word that you think is bottle.

danger great bottle
silly kite umbrella

Figure 1-5

6. Match the following capital and lower case letters by drawing a line between the ones that match. The first box is started for you. Trace over the dotted line. Match all the other letters in all four boxes by yourself.

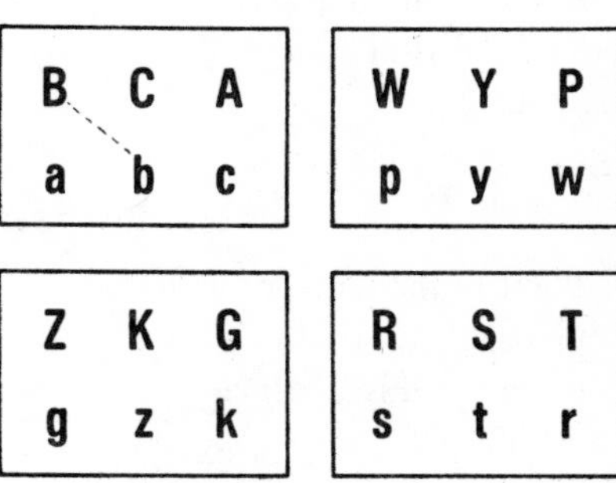

Figure 1-6

7. Look carefully! This time you have to watch out for

three things. See if you can find one word in which this letter—b—is the first letter, this letter—k—is the middle letter, and this letter—s—is the end letter of the word. Circle this word." (Leave the three letter cards in a wall chart as a reference.)

Figure 1-7

Raison d'Être

Children who can correctly mark exercises similar to the preceding ones understand that letters function in our written language as:

1. Parts of a name.
2. Beginnings of words.
3. Medial letters of words.
4. Ends of words.
5. Aids in finding a word among different words.
6. Aids in finding an unknown word.
7. Capital or lower case.

The second part of the test which follows assesses the child's concept of words.

READING READINESS TEST

Part II: Words

Oral Directions — *Children's Test Sheet*

1. "In this box are the names of all the children in this room. Find your name and circle it.

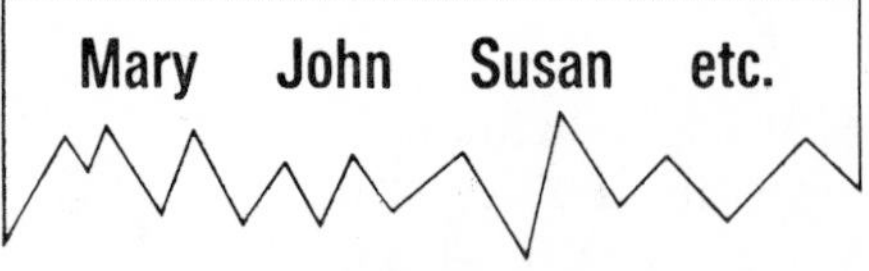

Figure 1-8

2. Point to the sentence with a number '1' in front of it. One word in this sentence is *see*. It looks like this—See (hold up the flash card for about one second). Circle the word *see*.

1. See the ball.

Figure 1-9

3. Point to the sentence with a '2' in front of it. A word in this sentence is *ball*. Look carefully while I hold up the word– ball . Circle the word *ball.*

4. Count the sentences in the next box. There are five of them. Look carefully while I hold up one of the sentences– See the ball. (Flash the sentence for about 5 seconds.) Circle the sentence that looks the same."

2. See the big ball.

Figure 1-10

A ball is big.
See the balloon.
See the ball.
What a red ball.
See the boy.

Figure 1-11

INVENTORY OF READING READINESS

When children do these exercises, they are not reading; they are matching word forms with a form carried in their visual memory. Children who correctly mark exercises similar to these understand how words function in our written language. They learn that words are:

1. Letters preceded and followed by a space.
2. Sometimes names.
3. Sometimes beginnings, middles, or ends of sentences.

They learn too, that words are forms that can be seen and matched even before they can be read. They learn that words are the building blocks of sentences.

At this stage, the child's curiosity about letters and words may reflect minimal exposure to them; in which case, the teacher is assessing the child's experiential background more than his attitude toward reading. If this were true, it would be necessary for her to bombard the child with such things as letters and words in color, in varying sizes, and in success-oriented games.

Children who are able to complete tasks similar to these without signs of pressure are ready for reading instruction. The ones who are not ready to do this can be taught to do it.

METHOD FOR INDIVIDUAL ASSESSMENT OF LEARNING

Of equal importance to the readiness assessment just presented is the need to find out the most efficient way to teach each child. Three commonly used methods of introducing words are by: sound, picture, and meaning association.

These methods are spoken of as points of emphasis rather than exclusive methods. The child needs to be taught to make use of all the clues that are available to him. Regardless of which methods are used, whether sound, picture, or meaning association, the teacher must be cognizant of the fact that there will be some overlapping.

The sound-association method is the slowest way to introduce words. On the other hand, if the child learns by this means only, it is the fastest method for him. The picture-association method also requires time and patience on the part of the teacher, but it is the most successful for certain children. The meaning-association method requires the least effort of the teacher, and the greatest amount of skill on the part of the student. Because of the many variations of learning patterns, it is important that the teacher know the individuals in her group so that she can fit the method to the child.

The *Mills Learning Methods Test*[4] can be used. There are, however, three features of this test that interfere with its popularity: (1) the test takes five days to complete; (2) words assessed as unfamiliar on the first day may be known by the fourth day; and (3) the time constant used in presenting the methods is difficult to hold to. Partly because of these disadvantages, and partly because the Mills Test may not be readily available to teachers, we are including an Informal Inventory of Methods. The test can be administered in one day and completed in five minutes on the following day. The structure of this Informal Inventory is balanced in the following four ways:

1. Each method of introduction includes words of comparable external difficulty.
2. No initial consonants are repeated.
3. No end consonants are repeated.
4. No phonograms are repeated.

---

[4] Robert E. Mills, "Learning Methods Test," The Mills Center, 1512 E. Broward Blvd., Fort Lauderdale, Florida, 1955.

Each method has one word fitting the basic CVC pattern: *can, pin, jar.* Each method has a word fitting a long-vowel pattern: *wait, bride, rope.* Each method has a word which ends in a digraph: *match, long, splash.* You may prefer to choose your own words of comparable design. It is important, however, that the words selected be unknown to the child.

The Pattern of Learning Test which follows will assess the child's ability to associate words with picture clues, meaning clues, and sound clues.

PATTERN OF LEARNING TEST

Friday Schedule:

Period I–First part of the morning:
Set I – 10 minutes–Teach
2-minute review

Period II–After recess:
3 minutes–Test Set I
Set II – 10 minutes–Teach
2-minute review

Period III–First period in the afternoon:
3 minutes–Test Set II
Set III – 10 minutes–Teach
2-minute review

Period IV–After the rest break:
3 minutes–Test Set III

Monday Schedule:

Period V–First part of the morning:
5 minutes–Retest all nine words in the order in which they were presented.

Chart 1-1

The sequence of presentation is included here in chart form (Chart 1-1) so that it will be easier to visualize the design. We vary the order of presentation in order to prevent biasing the results. By alternating the sequence of presentation, the reliability of the test is increased.

Notice that in presenting Set I (Figure 1-12), the picture-association, (PA), is first and begins with the word *can.* In Set II the meaning association, (MA), is first and begins with *long.* In Set III the sound association, (SA), is first and begins with *rope.*

SEQUENCE OF PRESENTATION

Order of Presentation	*Method Set I*	*Method Set II*	*Method Set III*
FIRST	(PA) can (CVC)	(MA) long (di)	(SA) rope (v)
SECOND	(MA) wait (v)	(SA) pin (CVC)	(PA) match (di)
THIRD	(SA) splash (di)	(PA) bride (v)	(MA) jar (CVC)
			vowel (v) consonant (c) digraph (di)

Figure 1-12

Each of the three sets will require 12 flash cards, a duplicated review sheet, two duplicated test sheets, and a pencil for each child. Since the material needed for each of the three sets is similar (although used in different sequence), we will list here only the detailed items needed for Set I.

Suggestions for Administering

Teach Set I

(A) *Picture Association* (Figure 1-13)–

1. Two large flash cards, one for boys and one for girls. On the right half print the word *can,* and on the left half put a picture of a can. This card should be creased

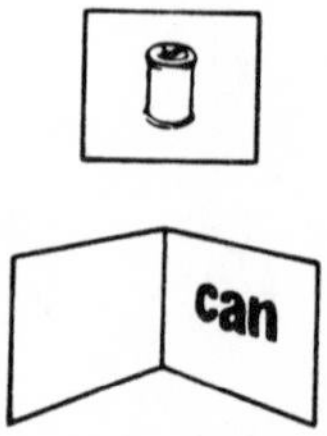

can

to fold in the middle so that the class may view one half at a time.

2. Flash card with the letters:

ca

3. Flash card with the letters:

Figure 1-13

(B) *Meaning Association* (Figure 1-14)–

1. Two flash cards (one for the boys, one for the girls) for the word *wait.* Each card pictures a child sitting in a chair, signifying that he has to wait for something.
2. Make two large cards in which the meaning of *wait* is depicted verbally and pictorially.

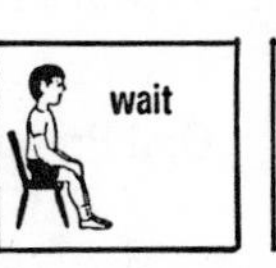

Figure 1-14

(C) *Sound Association* (Figure 1-15) –

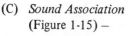

1. One flash card with:
2. One flash card with:
3. Two flash cards with:

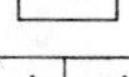

Figure 1-15

(D) *Review* –

Prepare a review sheet like that shown in Figure 1-16.

can
wait
splash

Figure 1-16

(E) *Recall*–

See Figure 1-17.

Oral Directions

Period 1: (12 minutes—early morning)

"Today I shall teach you three words that no one in the class knows how to read. Don't worry if they look hard. Look at them *very carefully*. Let's see how many of you can remember these words. First I shall show you a picture. Then I shall show you the word that goes with the picture."

Note: Spend approximately 3 minutes per word.

Picture Association (All picture associations are presented in approximately the same manner.)

Oral Presentation: "This is a picture of a *can* (or bride, or match.)

This is how the word *can* looks. (Unfold the flash card.)

can

How many letters does the word have? . . . Yes, that is right. There are three letters.

(Write several letters on the board.)

a o c b m n

Who can circle the first letter of the word can? . . .

Who can circle the second letter of the word can? . . .

Who can circle the last letter of the word? . . .

Use the next card

an

Is this the word can? . . .
What is missing? . . .

Next card

ca

Is this can? . . .
What is missing? . . ."

an

Mix and flash the four cards and ask the children to raise their hands when they see the written word *can*. Then have them say the word aloud.

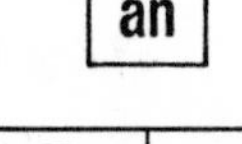

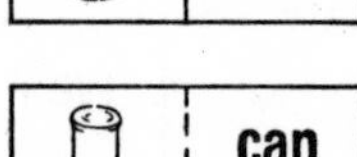

Individual Practice: Give one card with the picture and the word *can* to a girl, and one to a boy. Have each child say the word aloud, look at the picture, and then pass it on to the next girl (or boy) until all have had a turn.

Meaning Association (All meaning associations are presented in approximately the same manner.)

Oral Presentation: Hold up the card *wait* (or pin, or match).

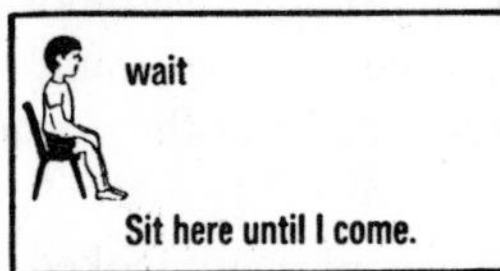

"This new word is *wait.* Do you wait for your mother to get breakfast? I sometimes have to wait for you to become quiet. Do you ever wait for me? . . . Do you ever wait for your friends on the playground? . . .

Can you use the word *wait* in a sentence?"

Individual Practice: "I will give this girl and this boy a card with the word *wait* on it. When it is your turn, say the word aloud, use it in a sentence, then pass it on to the next boy (girl) or until all have had a turn."

Sound Association (All sound associations are presented in approximately the same manner.)

Oral Presentation: Show the following flash cards:

spl

"These three letters sound like this: /spl/. Repeat the sound when I hold up the card. (practice)

ash

These three letters sound like this: /ash/. Say /ash/ when I hold up the card." (practice)

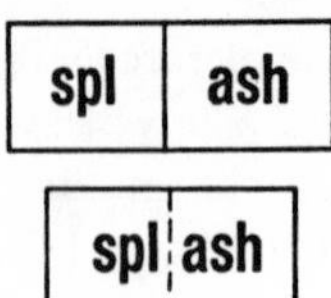

Practice mixing the two cards.

Now blend the sounds together like this (splash).

Flash the four cards spl, ash, splash, and spl/ash for speedy practice.

Individual Practice: Give one card with the word spl ⋮ ash to a girl and one to a boy. Have each child first sound the two halves of the word and then blend them to form the word.

Review: Distribute a duplicated sheet with all three words on it for a quick review. *See figure to left.* Say, "Remember how the word *wait* looked? See if you can find it. Put a circle around *wait.*" Teacher checks and helps those who are not correct.

can
wait
splash

"Remember how the word *splash* looked? See if you can find it. Draw a line under *splash.*

Remember how the word *can* looked? See if you can find it. Put a big X on *can*." Assist any child who needs help.

Collect the papers. Since this is an exercise for the purpose of reinforcing the words taught, the papers have no further value.

* * * *

Period 2: (15 minutes after recess)

Note to Teacher: The most effective way to determine whether the children learned the three words taught to them in the first period, is to flash the words to each child individually. If this individual testing is not feasible, distribute a duplicated test similar to the following:

Directions:

Write your name on the top of the paper or ask your teacher to do this. Point to the box with a picture of a can. Look carefully at each word. Four of the words in this box are *can*. Circle *can* every time you see it in this box. (Allow ample time before proceeding.)

Point to the box in the middle of the paper. Find and circle the word *wait* every time you see it. There are four of them.

TEST FOR SET I

		SCORE ______ Circle One
can	big can cat an at man can can can an	(PA) 0 25 50 75 100
wait	wait said we meat wait card sound wait wait want	(MA) 0 25 50 75 100
splash	splash splint splash on dash cash splash mash sash splash	(SA) 0 25 50 75 100

Figure 1-17

Point to the last box on the page. Find and circle *splash* every time you see it. There are four of them.

(Collect the papers. Score each section on a 100% basis. For example, a child could get a perfect score on picture association, 50% on sound association, and possibly nothing on meaning association. Results of this assessment of Set I comprise 1/6 of the composite score to be used as a comparative rating. File each child's test in an individual folder.)

Teach Set II Follow a format that is similar to the presentation in Set I. You will note that the sequence has been changed.

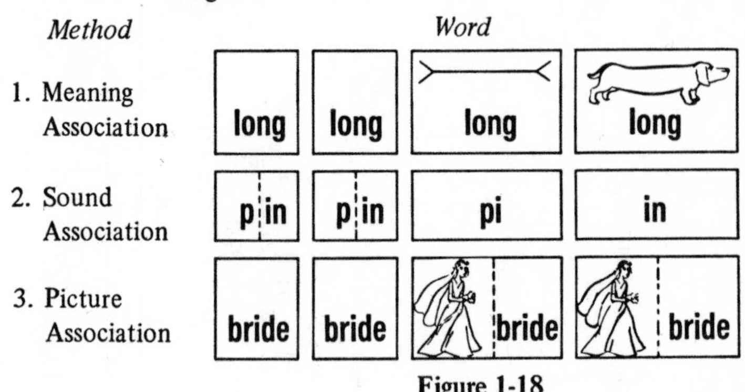

Figure 1-18

Review: Similar to directions for the first three words taught.

long
pin
bride

Figure 1-19

* * * *

Period 3: (15 minutes—early afternoon)

Test individually by class as before.

Score and file papers as before.

TEST FOR SET II

		Score ________
Circle *long* every time you see it.	song it long long wing long get to gnat long	(MA) 0 25 50 75 100
Circle *pin* every time you see it.	nap pin not put pin pat pin man pin is	(SA) 0 25 50 75 100
Circle *bride* every time you see it.	bride big side kite ride bump bride bride ride bride	(PA) 0 25 50 75 100

Figure 1-20

Teach Set III Follow format similar to presentation in Set I. You will note that the sequence has again been changed.

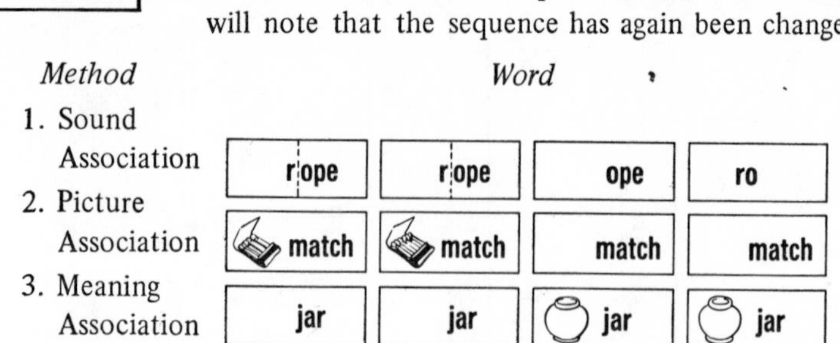

Figure 1-21

Review: Similar to directions for the first three words taught.

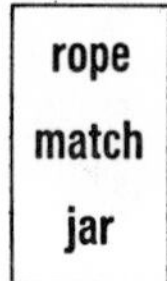

Figure 1-22

* * * *

Period 4: (3 minutes–late afternoon)

Test individually or by class as before.
Score and file.

At the end of these four periods, the teacher will have some measure of the child's ability to recall words which have been introduced by three different methods.

* * * *

Period 5: (3 minutes–Monday morning)

To check the child's *delayed recall,* test him individually on Monday morning. If individual testing is not feasible, give the class the same three group tests that were used on Friday. Give these tests in the same order in which they were originally presented; that is, Test for Set I, Set II, and Set III.

TEST FOR SET III

						Score				
Circle *rope* every time you see it.	dip	rope	road	pit	rope					(SA)
	hope	rope	deep	rope	and	0	25	50	75	100
Circle *match* every time you see it.	match	chat	match	match	mat					(PA)
	match	hatch	chair	little	latch	0	25	50	75	100
Circle *jar* every time you see it.	camp	bar	carry	see	jar					(MA)
	can	jar	jar	jar	cat	0	25	50	75	100

Figure 1-23

The words successfully remembered on Monday, as determined by the delayed-recall testing, give you the strongest clue as to the method most appropriate to teach the child. Keep individual cards on the children. Score on a percentage basis.

Children's patterns of learning change. Therefore, the teacher may want to give tests similar to these at intervals during the school year in order to determine whether there has been any change, and if so, the direction of the change. The following Periodic Progress Data Card is suggested for this purpose.

PERIODIC PROGRESS DATA CARD

BROWN, Barbara

Date Test I __________	Recall	Delayed Recall
1. Picture Association	____	____
2. Meaning Association	____	____
3. Sound Association	____	____
Date Test II __________		
1. Meaning Association	____	____
2. Sound Association	____	____
3. Picture Association	____	____
Date Test III __________		
1. Sound Association	____	____
2. Picture Association	____	____
3. Meaning Association	____	____

Try:

- bascal reading ☐
- creative writing ☐
- self-selection ☐

TOTAL PER CENT ACCURATE

P.A. ________

M.A. ________

S.A. ________

Figure 1-24

ANALYSIS ON WORDS LEARNED

Inherent in the three methods is the necessity for visually remembering the form of the word. In those cases where the child scored zero in words learned, when tested on delayed and short-term recall, stronger bonds of association need to be formed. Some children need the added sensory involvement of tracing or even to have the letters and words formed in three dimension. Chapters 10 and 12 offer additional suggestions on other methods and materials to be used with these children.

WORDS BY PICTURE ASSOCIATION

Children who learn best by picture association are well suited to a method that emphasizes a basal approach to reading. The advantage of this emphasis is that it strengthens the child's weak areas of sound and meaning association. At the same time, it utilizes the ability to recognize picture clues. The teacher can introduce the creative-writing approach to reading as the child becomes more skilled in sounding words. She can move into the self-selection area as the child becomes more skilled in associating sounds and meaning with words.

WORDS BY MEANING AND SOUND ASSOCIATION

Children who score well in both sound and meaning association are well suited to a program emphasizing a self-selection approach. These children enjoy figuring out new words on their own. When they encounter new words, they have two ways to check their accuracy in reading: by sound and meaning.

The children who learn equally well by all three introductions should be taught by the least time-consuming method. In most instances, this would be by the meaning-association emphasis. One aspect of this would be embedding an unknown word among known words, for example:

can
telephone
play
me

"One of the above words names the instrument you use to call up and talk to a friend." Since these children know the meaning of all other words in this list, the only remaining word is *telephone.* They then apply every clue available to the new word and in this way check their own accuracy. In general, these children are ready for a combination of the language-experience program and a program wherein the child learns to formulate his own generalizations, like Strand I and II of the Harper, Row Readers.

The intrinsic value of the Pattern of Learning Test is that it forces the teacher to take a close look at the way the child learns. Once we have established the learning pattern, we are able to select the method best suited for each child. And even more important, we avoid the damaging practice of subjecting an entire class to a single method in the mistaken assumption that it will be equally appropriate for every child in the class.

In conclusion, those of us who have been guilty of dealing with children as though they were proficient in word-attack skills are remiss in at least three ways:

1. In not using reading inventories to find out what the child does and does not know.
2. In treating all children as though they were from identical molds.
3. In assuming that all children beginning a complicated learning assignment were already masters of some aspects of it.

Basically, the beginning reader needs instruction. He must be able to associate spoken words with written words, learn the sound and structure of words, and read words from left to right.

2

IDENTIFYING KEY FACTORS IN READING

Children ordinarily learn to read when they are able to focus on print at near point, are curious about letters and words, and are interested in what words and letters stand for.

In this chapter we discuss traditional and modern views of readiness. The most complicated task of a lifetime is learning to speak. Can we apply any of the naturalness of learning to speak in learning to read? Can we amalgamate the factors in learning to read into a workable formula? The author believes we can.

There is nothing sacrosanct about the written word. Yet there is a tendency to accept it unequivocally. In the case of learning to read, for lack of a devil's advocate, we have unquestioningly adopted and promulgated traditional ideas advanced by early reading specialists. Conceived in good faith but formulated before sufficient research, these tenets have been reinforced by constant repetition and restatement. These tenets have also been strengthened by a pattern of success with many individuals, thus leading to overgeneralization.

TRADITIONAL WISDOM

Occasionally, it is wise to stand back and take an objective view of traditional wisdom. Conclusions drawn from 20 years' study of classroom and clinical data cause the author to question these long-accepted criteria. Among the commonly held beliefs that are being challenged are the following requisites for learning to read:

1. Near-average intelligence.
2. Long attention span.
3. Good muscle coordination.
4. Visual acuity.
5. Auditory acuity.
6. Physical maturity.
7. Ability to follow directions.
8. An expanded vocabulary adequate to communicate ideas and needs.
9. Emotional maturity.

Let us take a look at what the records show. Contrary to these popularly accepted tenets, it has been found that children in mental institutions and EMR (educable mentally retarded) classes can learn to read. Children considered hyperactive and classified as EH (educationally handicapped) have also learned to read. The same is true of those children with poor muscle coordination, poor vision or blindness, and those who are hard of hearing or deaf. Children who lack ability to follow directions can and often do teach themselves to read. An expanded vocabulary is not necessary, as it has been found that children with meager language facility have learned to read. (This is also apparent with adults who have no oral fluency in a foreign language and yet can learn to read it silently with comprehension.) And so we conclude that many of the traditional ideas advanced by pioneer reading specialists may justifiably be questioned. At least we may be more accurate in thinking of the nine points previously mentioned as attributes rather than prerequisites for reading.

Probably much more significant than the traditional beliefs is the discovery that normal children who read published books commonly exhibit the following characteristics: (1) the ability to focus on print at near point, (2) a curiosity about letters and words, and (3) an interest in reading. Let us consider these traditional factors individually.

VISION

It may seem contradictory to question good vision as a prerequisite for reading, and at the same time rate the ability to focus on print at near point as one of the three most important criteria in learning to read.

It has been shown, however, that even children with eye problems can learn to read. Faulty vision may contribute to headaches and fatigue, but according to Robinson's research,[1] it is rarely the primary cause of difficulty in learning to read. Faulty vision should be corrected by surgery, lenses, or exercise in order to lessen discomfort. Several tests help determine the effectiveness of the most important element of vision which influences the child's ability to read—the ability to focus at near point. One such test is the Keystone Visual Survey Test.[2] The section of that test devoted to near point is invaluable and frequently used in reading diagnoses. The far-point vision section of the test, while of some interest to the reading teacher, is more pertinent to other subject areas, such as outdoor sports.

LETTERS AND WORDS

Curiosity about letters and words is important as the leavening ingredient of learning to read. Based on the author's observation and experience, the most important fundamental need is to inculcate in the child an interest in letters and words. Our job is to stimulate this interest. This is not a new idea. Durrell's research in 1958[3] explored this phenomenon. Letter knowledge may be an outcome of the child's environment, in which adults place a high value on ABC books and education in general. Exposures of this kind develop the child's interest in these areas.

Regardless of the factors which kindle awareness of letters, interest in them is a necessary ingredient in learning to read. Children must recognize letters and distinguish one from another rapidly; further, they must establish relationships between sounds and symbols. I have yet to observe a child who learned to read without displaying these interests.

ISOMORPHIC PHENOMENA

The preschool children who learned to read before formal school instruction, as reported in Durkin's research,[4] most likely learned

---

[1] Helen M. Robinson, *Why Pupils Fail in Reading* (Chicago: University of Chicago Press, 1946), pp. 223-224.

[2] Keystone View Company, Meadville, Pennsylvania 16335.

[3] Donald D. Durrell, "Success in First Grade Reading," *Journal of Education,* Boston University School of Education, Vol. 140 (Feb. 1958).

[4] Delores Durkin, *Children Who Read Early* (New York: Bureau of Publications, Teachers College, Columbia University, 1966).

isomorphically. That is, they were able to distinguish words as being uniquely connected with words they had already heard and/or spoken.

According to linguists, the most complicated learning in a child's life is *learning to speak,* and yet this is achieved without conscious effort on his part. For most children, this seems a natural accomplishment. A baby literally stumbles on sound and is rewarded. As he gains control, he imitates sounds—and the day he imitates "mama" is a celebrated event.

Part of the naturalness of learning to speak is that "readiness" for speech surrounds the child. From the day of his birth, he is bombarded with speech sounds. Since readiness is encouragement to discover and experiment with the ingredients of learning, the baby's world is eminently geared to readiness for speech. The following six factors operate to facilitate this learning:

1. *Simplified Environment.* Adults hum, coo, and sustain a single pitch.
2. *Time.* There are no time limits or reporting periods. Time is not a threat but a commodity to be used.
3. *Operant Conditioning.*
   a. Adults reward the baby for any sounds he stumbles onto.
   b. The baby is rewarded for matching pitch and volume, and for duration of sound.
4. *Rich Environment.* The baby is surrounded by people using speech.
5. *Tutoring Situation.* The child has the full attention of one or more persons.
6. *Controlled Input.* Stimulation and rewards are given for a select word, such as "mama," before new words are taught.

Logically, these same factors could apply to the second most complicated learning, which is learning to read. A suggested application of the same components could proceed in this fashion:

Simplified Environment	In the case of learning to read, the simplified ingredients to be discovered and experimented with are printed letters, sounds, and eventually, words.
Time	Both the readiness and the actual learning could extend over a period of time that is comfortable to the individual. Goal expectancies could be set up for age ranges, but no limits established to report failures.
Operant Conditioning	In the classroom, a child can be rewarded for every correct response through the use of programmed and self-

correcting, independent work sheets. Structuring easy success steps is a vital part of operant conditioning.

Rich Environment

Children from homes where the family spends time reading are more likely to become effective readers. Classrooms, too, can provide a rich environment and may in some instances compensate for a lack of reading in the home. Teachers need the freedom to create this atmosphere by whatever means they choose. One teacher may be so highly selective in her books that she has only a few, and these achieve the stature of rare jewels. Another teacher may inundate the classroom with every conceivable bit of published matter, including coupons, flyers, and catalogues. This kind of material creates immediate value, especially when coupons are returned and the products received.

Tutorial Situation

The advantages of tutorial teaching are unquestioned. Expense is the deterrent. With imagination, we can set up tutorial classrooms at little or no extra cost. Schools are just beginning to explore paraprofessional volunteers—parents, retired school teachers, and other adults—who can be trained to follow through in small-group instruction.

Assuming there are no paraprofessionals available, there are other ways to conduct tutoring. Here is a diagram which shows how a teacher can multiply her effectiveness in teaching a slow-paced reading group.

Chain Tutoring

STEP 1. Teacher (T) selects the slowest-paced child (S^1) from the group. She introduces the vocabulary to him and tells the child to note *how* she does it so that he in turn can teach another child. $T \rightarrow S^1$

STEP 2. S^1 plays the role of the teacher. He teaches the vocabulary to another child (S^2) while teacher observes (T°). $T^\circ (S^1 \rightarrow S^2)$

STEP 3. Now, you have two student teachers (S^1, S^2) who teach two other children (S^3, S^4) from the group. $(S^1 \rightarrow S^3)$ $(S^2 \rightarrow S^4)$

STEP 4. By STEP 4, you have four student teachers.

STEP 5. Have the four pairs of children read the story in whatever manner you consider appropriate. For example, have the student teacher in each pair read aloud until she can tell what the unresolved problem of the story is. Then, have the other child in each pair read until the end of the story, or the pairs of children read simultaneously, in the manner of the historical "blab" school.

By selecting the slowest-paced child first, the teacher is doing the teaching and the student who needs it the most is having an opportunity for meaningful practice. Not the least advantage is the self-confidence this child builds as he, in turn, succeeds in the role of the teacher.

Controlled Input

It may well be that controlled input in all *initial* learning is the most important single factor responsible for success. One of the primary reasons for controlled input is to avoid frustration. Many people have been baffled upon hearing an unfamiliar language spoken by natives. A similar frustration is experienced by those children who are "locked into" such a fast-paced reading program that they are overwhelmed by their inability to keep up. Such an impossible situation can easily create an attitude of defeat through failure. Lack of control in the beginning stages of reading is the "Achilles Heel" of the creative writing-to-reading and individualized reading programs. Oddly enough, it is this same lack of control that becomes the strength of both programs *after* the vocabulary skill development essentials are covered. Once the child has these vocabulary skills, programs that provide an opportunity to apply them (without putting any ceiling on the words) are superior to restrictive programs.

NEUROLOGICAL FUNCTIONING

Centralized processing is the most important (and at the same time the least known) function of the manner in which learning takes place in the individual. Anatomically, the network of nerves serves as analyzers, conveyors, summators, and inhibitors of learning. For a full century, scientists have been trying to localize data-processing regions in the brain. While it is generally agreed that the controls for one side of the body are located on the opposite hemisphere of the brain, there is little else of consensus. One of the newer attempts to map control centers in the brain is through observation of patients during surgically exposed cortex stimulation.

Even though we cannot pinpoint central processing biologically and functionally, we have evidence that it occurs. Subjects completely immobilized by a curare-like drug,[5] while incapable of muscular activity, were able to perceive and remember thinking activities. While this provides some evidence that thinking is a central rather than a peripheral activity, neurologists are still no closer to specifying the locale or the mechanics of the way thinking occurs.

Since we are not permitted the luxury of being able to pinpoint and directly stimulate a reading-learning center, we can only attempt to assemble a workable formula from what we now know about reading.

In setting up this formula, it is vital to measure the ease with which a child learns a particular word. No matter how well he appears to read, in the final analysis, if he cannot distinguish one word from another, he is not truly "reading" by any common definition of the term. Therefore, our primary concern in studying a beginning reader is to note the ease with which the child can match the printed word with the spoken word.

As we cannot trace the physiological decoding of a word, we can only hypothesize on the basis of empirical evidence. The learning of a word by a child involves the presence of three factors:

1. The ability to connect isomorphically written symbols with the word known in speech.
2. The ability to read written symbols which are not yet part of the child's speech and which may or may not be pronounceable by him.
3. The drive to do so.

READING FORMULA

The following formula is set up for the purpose of exploring relationships involved in the ease of learning to read a word:

Internal Processes (Int) multiplied by External Factors (Ext)
Multiplied by Motivation (M) equals Ease of Learning (E_L).

$$(\text{Int} \times \text{Ext} \times \text{M}) = E_L$$

Int: Refers to all internal happenings. Specifically, the word presented cannot be below the child's threshold of seeing and hearing. The neurological

[5] John Carroll, *Language and Thought* (Englewood Cliffs, N.J.: Prentice-Hall, Inc., 1964), p. 77.

system must transmit impulses to and from the point where processing of data takes place. The reservoir of knowledge for the beginning reader consists mainly of the stored speech words which are available to be connected isomorphically to the written symbols.

Ext: Refers to all external happenings. Specifically, difficulties arise which may be inherent in the word form, such as configuration confusion (can, car; then, than). Unpredictable sounds, such as *though, cough,* and *thought,* add greatly to the difficulty. Words outside the child's speech storehouse or known words with new meanings are foreign to the child.

M: Refers to the child's inner drive or motivation to learn a particular word. Motivation affects both internal and external forces.

Optimum scoring works as follows: a value of 20 has been arbitrarily assigned as a rating for the most desirable internal measures and a value of 10 for the external measures of a particular child. Motivation, however, is expressed in decimal fractions–with .5 as the optimum rating. Thus, the best possible product of 100, results from the formula (20 × 10 × .5 = 100) and indicates the child will learn the word with ease–probably on the first presentation.

As the child encounters *internal* difficulties in perceiving a word, the score becomes lower, to the lowest possible score of 0. In a similar direction, the *external* measures decrease with difficulty to 1. As *motivation* to learn a word lessens, the value assigned it diminishes to infinity.

So for the pupil who experiences a great deal of difficulty in internal processing, external factors, and motivation, the formula could look like this (1 × 1 × .1 = .1). Since the numbers were arbitrarily assigned, we cannot say that the word to be learned will have to be presented *n* number of times. We can only say that as factors interfere with learning, the product decreases, and chances of learning the word decrease.

The following three tables aid us in studying the interrelatedness of forces that facilitate or obstruct learning.

INTERNAL FACTORS IN LEARNING A WORD

Area	*Measurement of*	*Measured by*
Sensory Inadequacies	Outside Visual Threshold (Visual acuity)	Ophthalmologist
	Outside Auditory Threshold (Auditory acuity)	Audiologist

Area	*Measurement of*	*Measured by*
	Eye-Hand Coordination (as kinesthetic-sensory involvement is needed)	Bender-Gestalt[6] Getman Manual[7]
Neurological	Impulse Transmission (inadequate summation inhibition)	Neurologist
	Central Processing	Illinois Test of Psycholinguistic Abilities (I.T.P.A.)[8]
Academic Inadequacies	Insufficient Reservoir of Knowledge	(WISC)[9] Formal or Informal Tests

EXTERNAL FACTORS IN LEARNING A WORD

Insufficient configuration clues, as in minimal pairs:	can–car so–no
Unpredictable sound clues as in:	though, cough, thought
Unusual words:	syzygy, unicorn
New meanings for old words:	a *run*-in to *run* for office a *run* for your money a *run* in your socks

MOTIVATIONAL FACTORS IN LEARNING A WORD

Forces Competing for Attention	*Examples*
Primary Drives	hunger thirst pain body functions

[6] The Psychological Corporation, 304 East 45th Street, New York, N.Y. 10017.

[7] G. N. Getman and Elmer R. Kane, *The Physiology of Readiness* (Minneapolis: Programs to Accelerate School Success, Inc., 1964).

[8] The University of Illinois Press, Urbana, Illinois 61901.

[9] The Psychological Corporation, 304 East 45th Street, New York, N.Y. 10017.

Forces Competing for Attention	*Examples*
Behavior Controlled by Value System	desire to please desire to obey desire to respect desire to hurt

Familiarity with the formula and the preceding tables should heighten the teacher's awareness of the complicated factors involved in such an apparently simple task as learning one single word.

Since professional services are not always available, the following suggestions can be used by the teacher for screening, and as a guide for learning activities.

Internal Factors

1. Is the word seen by the child at near point? For a small percentage of children, this means reading from sight-saving books or books written in graduated sizes of print. Ask the child to read sentences of comparable difficulty from these books and watch for signs of eye strain.
2. Have the children in your reading circle sit with their backs toward you. Dictate a word to be repeated by the first child; another word for the second child; and continue with a word for each child in the group. Dictate the words, utilizing the same rate and volume that you ordinarily use. Observe which children find it necessary to have words repeated.
3. For those children who learn by seeing, saying, and tracing a word, we need measures of eye-hand coordination. These we can get by asking the child to connect widely separated dots with straight lines, trace over the resulting geometric forms, and copy the forms.
4. Children with different metabolic rates react at varying speeds. A very intelligent child may have a slow reaction time, while a moron may have a fast reaction time. A measure of reaction-recognition time is obtained by handing out a sheet with words for the children to underline. Flash word cards at 1/40 of a second and then at 1/2 a second, and observe which children respond correctly at each speed. The slowest child in the group sets the pace.
5. The teacher can get a measurement of the student's reaction time involving central processing by having the child give the opposite to a stimulus word presented. The stimulus words can be given both visually and orally.

6. Academic inadequacies can be measured by a Binet[10] or a Wechsler-Bellevue Intelligence Test (WISC). In particular, the first verbal subtest of the WISC will indicate whether the child has as much information as most children of his age. Young children are expected to be able to count, read a calendar, know the names of the days of the week, the number of days in a week, the months of the year, the four seasons of the year, and common objects around home and school.

External Factors

1. The child who is introduced to reading by whole words will need to be taught how to analyze minimal pairs, such as *cat* and *rat*. The child who has been taught to synthesize sounds will already have had experience with minimal pairs.
2. The child, when taught patterns of words, is helped to make the correct phoneme-to-grapheme association, as in: night, fight, right, light, blight, and fright.
3. When the child encounters an unusual word, he needs to use context clues to sound out the new word. He can be given practice in this skill by having the teacher introduce one prestige word a day. The prestige word should be a word unknown to any of the children, but one of interest to them. If you plan to read Thurber's *Unicorn in the Garden,*[11] you can put this sentence on the board:

   Is the unicorn an animal?
4. "Multiple meanings of words" is an important concept for the child to learn. Even in the primary grades the child learns that *play* can refer to having fun and to stories acted out.

Motivation

Children driven by primary needs are unresponsive to instruction. In most cases, their attention is so focused on a basic need that they have no attention left over. Acute hunger, extreme thirst, and violent body pain direct all the child's energy toward attending to basic needs.

Next, the voices competing for the child's attention are ranked

---

[10] Houghton Mifflin Company, Boston, Massachusetts 02107.

[11] James Thurber, *Fables for Our Times* (New York: Harper & Bros., 1939), pp. 65-66.

according to his personal value system. His culture, and especially the primary unit of which he is a member, contribute toward establishing his values. He has been taught to value the following in somc preferred order:

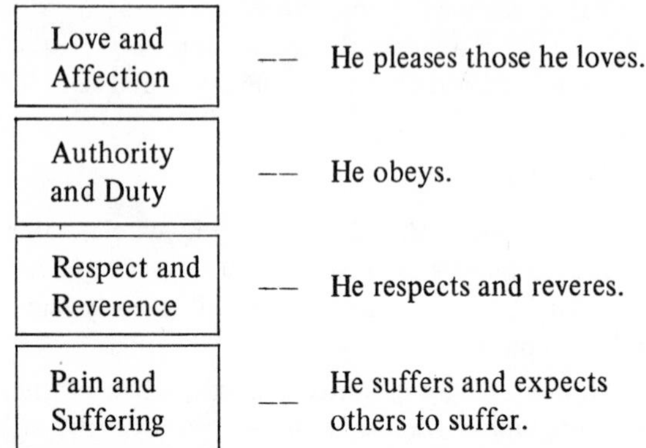

Love and Affection
— He pleases those he loves.
Authority and Duty
— He obeys.
Respect and Reverence
— He respects and reveres.
Pain and Suffering
— He suffers and expects others to suffer.

The child who has no respect for people, property, and conformity is badly equipped to fit into a regular classroom. In order to be receptive to instruction, the child must first place enough value on conformity to become a responsive learner.

It is well to remember that children are at all times motivated in one way or another. A child who is motivated to do nothing academically becomes less of a personal affront when we realize this response is the result of his value system. It is the value system that must be our concern. This will be discussed in Chapter 9.

3

DEVELOPING INSTRUMENTS FOR EXPLORATION

Evaluating students one-at-a-time is crucial to individualizing a reading program. Unless a teacher can give an individual test and satisfactorily diagnose one student, it is unlikely she can evaluate a classroom of students.

This chapter is based on the premise that teachers who plan to individualize instruction need to develop skill in administering tests to individuals. Results of group tests are, at best, an unknown quantity and at worst, misleading.

The instruments for exploration that follow are simple enough to be made up by the teacher, or they may be copied as they appear in this book. All of the instruments included here are oral and therefore must be individually administered. The Wide Range Achievement Test (WRAT)[1] is the only standardized instrument referred to.

Reading problems occur with the unpredictableness of a childhood contagion. It is difficult to comprehend why children exposed to the same contagion are not all equally susceptible to a disease. In a similar manner, it is also difficult for a layman to understand why identical treatment of children results in some who learn to read and others who do not. In both cases, it is urgent that we treat the symptoms immediately or risk permanent damage to the afflicted. No physician would subject a child with measles to a lengthy exposure of bright lights and drafts while he collected data

[1]The Psychological Corporation, 304 East 45th Street, New York, N.Y. 10017.

from past history. After verified diagnosis, he would instead begin immediate treatment of the symptoms. In the case of the child with reading problems, he too needs immediate diagnosis and treatment. His psychological welfare is equally as much in jeopardy as the physiological condition of the child with measles.

REALITY THERAPY IN READING

We suggest borrowing the reality therapy approach in working with troubled readers. Glasser[2] in his book on reality therapy points out the fruitlessness of a clinical psychologist's probing through past trauma. He makes a strong case for dealing with his client's problems as they exist at that moment in time. The technique strips the client of his shelter of *blame* and forces him to accept some responsibility for his own actions. In a similar manner, reading diagnosis begins with an assessment of present conditions rather than a lengthy probing for the causes that produced them. We deliberately avoid this blind alley because the process of uncovering the causes is time consuming, and because the past cannot be changed. It is possible that a well-intentioned diagnostician could be so intent upon completing a thorough diagnosis of causes that the actual treatment would be hopelessly delayed. The longer the treatment is postponed the less accurate is the interpretation, since the picture is constantly changing and the original findings may no longer be applicable. One can only alter what is happening right now or what will happen in the future, and it is important for the reader already in trouble to break the pattern of failure as soon as possible.

To do this, the teacher must become a diagnostician. Daily diagnosis is an outgrowth of learning to administer individual tests proficiently. The skill of diagnosis sensitizes the teacher to observe the effort made by the child in terms of nervous energy, as well as to note the correctness of the child's answers. Some other advantages of individually administered reading tests are:

1. Informal inventories to administer individually are on hand for use by all teachers and at no additional expense.
2. Observations of the child's behavior during the test are frequently as valuable as the record of his performance. The teacher gains a greater

[2] William Glasser, M.D., *Reality Therapy: A New Approach to Psychiatry* (New York: Harper & Row, 1965).

insight into the manner in which the child functions, the child's academic knowledge, the speed and confidence of his response, and his tolerance of failure.

3. The child has the undivided attention of an adult, and this gives him a feeling of worth.
4. The child shows the teacher what he *can* do, and upon completion of the test, he is assured of help with what he cannot do.
5. All diagnosis must eventually be individual, and by testing the child alone the teacher can pinpoint the child's specific needs with greater accuracy.

Effective diagnosis deals with the here-and-now in the most positive way possible.

The author favors individually administered reading tests. It is hoped that in the future all teachers will be required to administer individual rather than group tests, thus insuring more accurate evaluation. Reading texts applaud the desirability of ongoing diagnosis, but this is seldom found in the classroom since so few teachers are trained to administer and interpret individual tests. Unless a teacher is trained to assess one child at a time, she has no starting point for ongoing diagnosis.

Individually administered tests are also less frustrating for the child. In this type of test, it is not necessary to subject the child to repeated failure in order to ascertain the test ceiling. In an individual test, such as a graded word list, the teacher is able to start by giving the child successful experiences. As the test progresses, the child is encouraged to tell which words or parts of words he knows. The emphasis is on what the child knows (or thinks he knows) rather than on what he doesn't know. The positive approach is continued until the ceiling is reached. Even at this point, the teacher continues to encourage the child to attempt to identify words or parts of words in any of the remaining lines.

In contrast to the individual test, the child who takes a 30-minute group test may have a ceiling lower than the simplest test item. In a case such as this, the child is required to sit through a half hour of unrelieved frustration.

The Law of Parsimony applies to the selection of tests. A principle to guide in selecting the instrument to be used for exploring is: Select the fastest and least threatening tests for the pupil with the most severe reading problems. The need for assessment is not confined to any specific grade or age but may be administered wherever needed.

SPONTANEOUS WORD LIST

Regardless of chronological age, the simplest and least threatening reading test is the "Spontaneous Word List." In this test the teacher says, "Write your name and any other words that you know." Usually a few minutes of time are enough. The test is appropriate to administer to any pupil who has *n* number of years of schooling, but who has learned little else than his name. The test cannot be failed. Accept the words written, no matter how the student spells them. Words other than the student's name are likely to be words he has overlearned. This gives you a nucleus of known words. Therefore, at this point, you have in a matter of minutes established a basis for beginning success-oriented instruction. Utilize what he has written to build new words from known parts.

Example:

Spontaneous Word List

Brad wrote these words: Brad
is
the
stop

From this list the teacher could build new words in sets of three, such as: st, br blends and op, ad rhyming endings:

st*op*	*st*op	*Br*ad	Br*ad*
h*op*	*stay*	*br*ave	l*ad*
p*op*	*st*ing	*br*ing	d*ad*

or in sets of two with the initial digraph th, and the rhyming of is and his:

*th*e	*is*
*th*at	h*is*

Phrases in sets of these, such as:

Brave Brad
Brave Dad
Brave lad

Multiple meanings, such as:

Brad is a boy.
That is a brad. 

Dad is Pop.
That is pop. 

Sentences, such as:

Is the lad Brad?
The lad is Brad.
Brad is the lad.

Teach a new word both by sound and by context. Choice of new words should be based on what the pupil already knows and should also be geared to the book you select for him to read. Remember that the *first* poem or story that a child is expected to read should consist of words he has learned well or overlearned. It is vital to associate books with success. One way to insure a student's success in reading a book is to be sure that he is familiar with the vocabulary before he is expected to make use of it.

TOP TEN TEST

Another test which is very simple and quick to administer is the "Top Ten Test." This consists of high-frequency words and is appropriate to administer to a child entering the classroom when little is known about his reading ability.

Top Ten Test

a	in
and	the
for	to
of	we
I	you

It is important to remember that in this test the child probably has not overlearned these words. All you are asking him to do is identify words already printed; consequently, you cannot consider that he has mastered these words, even though he may be able to read all of them correctly once.

Introduce the test by saying, "The following list contains ten words that look easy, but they are surprisingly hard to learn. You cannot draw pictures of them or act them out. If you think you know one, point to it." By suggesting that the list is considered a difficult one, you take the pressure off the pupil who does not know any of the words. If the child doesn't know any of them, do not attempt to teach each word as an isolated element. Select those words from the preceding list that are to be found first in the text the child will be reading. Use these words in conjunction with the child's name and personal experience as much as possible. For the child who knows all the words, point out how often these words occur and how valuable they are, by letting him count the number of times he can find them in an adult book, newspaper, or magazine.

We have now discussed two of the simplest diagnostic instruments available; that is, the student's "Spontaneous Word List" and the "Top Ten Test List." But for students who have already learned 30 or more words, these two tests are not appropriate. We need other instruments, such as graded word lists and informal oral reading inventories.

GRADED WORD LIST

One advantage of a graded word list is that any teacher can make up one of her own. All that is needed is a set of basal readers, preferably one not currently read by the students. From the back of the book, select every *nth* word that is new to that book until ten words have been selected from each level of difficulty. Omit all proper nouns. Write each list of ten words on a 5 × 7 card. The test is administered in a manner similar to the San Diego Quick Assessment, which follows.

For the teacher who prefers a graded word list already compiled, we suggest the Queen's College list given in Harris[3] or the San Diego Quick Assessment which is printed here in its entirety:

Directions: Reading Readiness–

RR[1]–Be sure the child understands what *alike* and *different* mean. Then ask if each pair of letters is alike or different.

RR[2]–"How many of these letters can you correctly name?"

RR[3]–"Circle the letter you think this word begins with–"

Directions: Preprimer Through II

"There are ten words on each card. I would like you to try every word on this card. If you *think out loud,* I can tell which parts of the word you already know. After the test, I will help you with the parts you didn't know."

---

[3]Albert J. Harris, *How to Increase Reading Ability,* 5th ed. (New York: McKay, 1970), pp. 177-179.

SAN DIEGO QUICK ASSESSMENT

RR[1] *Matching Level (Alike or different)*		*RR*[2] *Reading Readiness Level (Letter names)*	*RR*[3] *Reading Readiness ("Circle the letter you think this word begins with–")*			
B	B	B	D	B	A	(bird)
A	C	A	A	E	K	(apron)
M	M	M	L	F	M	(mom)
C	C	C	B	C	G	(car)
S	Q	S	O	S	P	(sad)
J	J	J	A	B	J	(jeep)
T	T	T	D	G	T	(tag)
H	H	H	A	H	B	(house)
D	L	D	D	I	M	(door)
W	M	W	W	G	J	(wig)

* * * *

PP	*Primer*	*1*	*2*
see	you	road	our
play	come	live	please
me	not	thank	myself
at	with	when	town
run	jump	bigger	early
go	help	how	send
and	is	always	wide
look	work	night	believe
can	are	spring	quietly
here	this	today	carefully

3	*4*	*5*	*6*
city	decided	scanty	bridge
middle	served	business	commercial
moment	amazed	develop	abolish
frightened	silent	considered	trucker
exclaimed	wrecked	discussed	apparatus
several	improved	behaved	elementary
lonely	certainly	splendid	comment
drew	entered	acquainted	necessity
since	realized	escaped	gallery
straight	interrupted	grim	relativity

7	*8*	*9*	*10*	*11*
amber	capacious	conscientious	zany	galore
dominion	limitation	isolation	jerkin	rotunda
sundry	pretext	molecule	nausea	capitalism
capillary	intrigue	ritual	gratuitous	prevaricate
impetuous	delusion	momentous	linear	risible
blight	immaculate	vulnerable	inept	exonerate
wrest	ascent	kinship	legality	superannuate
enumerate	acrid	conservatism	aspen	luxuriate
daunted	binocular	jaunty	amnesty	piebald
condescend	embankment	inventive	barometer	crunch

This test can be used with those students who are not yet able to read, as well as those who read through grade 11. An analysis of their substitutions is drawn from the position and type of errors.

The pupil's grade level is ascertained by noting the grade level on which the child misses two or more words. To be sure that this is not a happenstance, it is recommended that the child be asked to see if he knows any words in the list a grade level beyond the one in which he missed two words. The following is a sample test protocol:

Error Analysis of
San Diego Quick Assessment

NAME John DATE 10/14

Score Key:

Position Errors

(I) *Initial*—Errors in initial consonants, blends, digraphs, and the first syllable of words with three or more syllables.

(M) *Medial*—Errors in the middle letters of a one-syllable word, or middle syllables of a word with three or more syllables.

(F) *Final*—Errors in final consonants, blends, digraphs, and last syllables of three or more syllable words.

Type of Error:

1. reversal
2. consonant
3. consonant cluster
4. short vowel
5. long vowel
6. digraph
7. prefix
8. suffix
9. root word
10. miscellaneous

Circle grade level in which all words are correctly read.

PP	(Pr)	1	2	3	4	5
6	7	8	9	10	11	

Grade Failed 3 Total Words Correct 44
(Give credit for all words below the basal.*)

Failed AT	Grade Level	Stimulus Word	Substitution Word	Position	Type
	1	always	away	I	2
	2	quietly	quickly	M	9
X	3	middle	muddle	M	4
	3	exclaimed	explained	M	9
	3	straight	street	M	5

*The basal level is the lowest grade level at which all *words* were correctly *pronounced.*

COMMENTS: John slowed down on the third-grade list. He sounded out the words *moment, frightened,* and *several* as though he had never read them before. He has the ability to sound out new words and to begin and end words correctly. None of his substitutions were nonwords. He sounds to recall words known to him in speech and therefore is aware of the *sense* as well as the sound of words.

RECOMMENDATIONS: He needs help on the first syllable *al* when combined with words such as already, although, and altogether. The root word *quiet* should be taught. The short sound of *i* as in *it* and *little,* as well as in *riddle* and *fiddle* should also be stressed. The word *aim* should be taught as well as the long *a* sound in rain, pain, and gain.

Root words and the pattern words should be taught in conjunction with known words. By using the words in phrases and sentences, the child learns to transfer his word knowledge into the act of reading.

The teacher will get leading clues about the pupil's feeling for words, based on his behavior—whether he is afraid of making an error, or whether he is overconfident and miscalls words without knowing he is wrong. Subjective evaluations are often as revealing as objective measurements.

WORD MEANINGS

An informal test of opposites can be developed by the teacher in much the same way as the graded word lists previously discussed. The advantage of a "word opposite test" is that the child must know more about a word than just how to pronounce it. He must know something about word meanings.

The test is appropriate to administer to a child whose comprehension is poor. The score will tell you if his weakness is due to lack of knowledge of word relationships. Opposites are related. For example, *dislikes* and *likes* both are measures of feeling, they are equidistant from a neutral central point, equidistant from the extremities along a continuum from hate to love, and they are typically used to describe the feelings of animate beings rather than inanimate objects.

The key words in this test are read *by the teacher* and can be more difficult than the words the child reads, as when the teacher reads the word *dislikes* and the child selects the word *likes.* The child is given a list of words selected by the teacher from the basal readers. The child has three words to choose from and must choose the one with the opposite meaning to the stimulus word.

San Diego Graded Word Opposites

Here are some typical examples of word opposites:

Teacher says:	*Child reads silently and selects:*	
Sample: walk	go (run) [circled] see	Primer Level
1. dislikes	likes jump look	
2. stand	see was sit	
3. down	you at up	
4. little	boy big bad	
5. out	in its is	

6. came — was / went / were
7. unhappy — happy / house / have
8. went — candy / car / came

FIRST LEVEL

Sample: throw — call / car / (catch)

1. girls	bump	boys	baby
2. slower	faster	seesaw	hop
3. man	pole	window	woman
4. pick up	drop	step	bear
5. hers	foot	his	rain
6. can	never	catch	cannot
7. lost	button	found	jingle
8. night	give	across	day

SECOND LEVEL

Sample: night — (day) / dark / down

1. square	rosy	round	read
2. last	fist	fast	first
3. left	red	right	round
4. dark	light	low	leave
5. noisy	still	stand	silly
6. close	oven	over	open
7. back	from	front	free
8. fearless	after	over	afraid

THIRD LEVEL

Sample: heavy — dark / (light) / black

1. goodbye	hello	help	hold
2. rough	gone	garage	gentle
3. soft	had	head	hard
4. serious	squeal	silly	jeep

5. asleep	awake	away	always
6. east	with	west	word
7. more	less	lead	load
8. sat	said	stood	was

FOURTH LEVEL

Sample: north — east / said / (south)

1. remember	fierce	ferry	forget
2. roughly	stride	smoothly	slope
3. false	trial	throb	true
4. queen	king	kept	kite
5. shy	bold	bad	burn
6. most	level	least	ledge
7. yours	maybe	me	mine
8. unable	able	art	after

FIFTH LEVEL

Sample: fat — slow / (slender) / spew

1. real	flat	fake	tough
2. exit	scout	ancient	entrance
3. outer	inner	flow	ramps
4. weak	folks	model	strong
5. dried	soaked	scoop	hedge
6. wonderful	details	awful	awkward
7. indirect	firm	queer	direct
8. incorrect	correct	witness	praised

The scoring is also similar to the graded word list. The child who gets one out of ten responses wrong passes that grade level. The child who misses two out of ten does not pass at that grade level. To be sure, try the next level and ask him if there are any words he recognizes or would like to try. Then read him the stimulus word to see if he can select the opposite from among the three words.

WIDE RANGE ACHIEVEMENT TEST

The Wide Range Achievement Test (WRAT) is an individually administered, standardized test for use in reading programs, clinics, and research. The 1965 edition has subtests in two levels. Level I can be used with children 5 years, 0 months through 11 years, 11 months. Level II is appropriate for use with persons 12 years, 0 months to adulthood. The three subtests include reading, spelling, and arithmetic, and the entire test takes from 20 to 30 minutes to administer. One of the advantages of these tests is that it is almost impossible to receive a score of zero, and for the child's self-esteem this is helpful–for research purposes it is vital. An academically impoverished pupil can receive a positive score in reading for being able to match letters, a positive score in spelling for being able to copy marks, and a positive score in arithmetic by being able to count dots.

It is suggested that you extend the manual directions to include recording the child's substitutions in reading by writing down the words substituted on the test sheet. It is diagnostically more important to classify the types of errors made than it is to note the number of errors made.

SAN DIEGO QUICK ORAL INVENTORY

The San Diego Quick Oral Inventory is an individually administered diagnostic test. It is appropriate to administer to persons known to have a reading level below grade five. Each of the nine cards contains short sentences made up of approximately 20 words written at one grade level. Each card contains some dialogue and must be read aloud by the student. His interpretation is often an indication of his comprehension. When he finishes reading, the teacher takes the card. She asks him how many things he can recall. If he cannot recall at least three items, use the suggested questions to help him recall. Begin testing at a lower level than the estimated reading level of the student.

San Diego Quick Oral Inventory

Scoring

Accuracy: The child who misses no more than three words on a card passes the accuracy of words in context at that grade level. It is helpful to write down the substitutions that the child makes.

Comprehension: The child who correctly remembers three items, whether or not he is prompted by questions, passes the comprehension at that grade level.

Note: Encourage the child to try all words, even if he is unsure of them. When he incorrectly says the word, give him the correct version so that he will have a chance to comprehend what he has read.

Preprimer Level

Teacher says: "Read about a boy and something he likes. Try to remember what you read."

> The boy looked at a toy.
>
> The toy is a big red *airplane*. 
>
> I like red *airplanes*.
>
> I can be happy.

Facts Remembered	*Questions, if Needed*
About a boy	(1. Who was the story about?)
Looked at a toy	(2. What did he see?)
It was a big red airplane	(3. What was the toy?)
He liked red airplanes	(4. What did he like?)
He felt happy	(5. How did he feel?)

First-Grade Level

Teacher says: "Read about a sad boy. Try to remember what you read."

> How sad the boy is now.
>
> His toy boat cannot be found.
>
> Mother said, "Ask for a new one
>
> for your birthday."

Teacher says: "Tell me as much as you can remember."

Facts Remembered	*Questions, if Needed*
A boy	(1. Who is it about?)
He is sad	(2. How does the boy feel?)
His toy boat is lost	(3. Why?)
His mother has an idea	(4. Who has a good idea?)
To ask for a new one	(5. What was it?)
For his birthday	(6. When?)

Second Grade–First Half

Teacher says: "Read about something funny that happened to Pat. Try to remember what you read."

> Pat woke up.
>
> He walked to school.
>
> No one was at school.
>
> "This is not a school day,"
>
> said Pat.

Teacher: "Tell me as much as you can remember."

Facts Remembered	*Questions, if Needed*
Pat	(1. Who did you read about?)
He woke up	(2. What happened first?)
He walked to school	(3. What next?)
No one was there	(4. What was unusual?)
It was not a school day	(5. What did Pat figure out?)

Second Grade–Second Half

Teacher says: "Read about Bob's surprise. Try to remember what you read."

> Bob walked into the big house.
>
> Suddenly, "Surprise!" shouted all the
>
> neighbors.
>
> "We waited for you to have a party."

Teacher: "Tell me as much as you can remember."

Facts Remembered	*Questions, if Needed*
Bob	(1. Who did you read about?)
Into the big house	(2. Where did Pat walk?)
Surprise	(3. Suddenly, what did Pat hear?)
The neighbors shouted	(4. Who said this?)
To have a party	(5. Why were the neighbors waiting?)

Third-Grade Level

Teacher says: "Read about Mike's huge box. Try to remember what you read."

> Mike got wonderful presents.
>
> Finally only one huge box remained.
>
> "It will be your favorite gift,"
>
> his friend suggested excitedly.

Teacher: "Tell me as much as you can remember."

Facts Remembered	*Questions, if Needed*
Mike	(1. Who is this about?)
He got wonderful gifts	(2. What kind of gifts did he get?)
Finally he had a huge box	(3. What finally remained?)
It would be Mike's favorite gift.	(4. What did Mike's friend think about the box?)

Fourth-Grade Level

Teacher says: "Read about Jim and the universe. Try to remember what you read."

> Jim studies the universe.
>
> "You mean the stars are suns?
>
> Then are other planets orbiting them?"
>
> he asked in disbelief.

Teacher: "Tell me as much as you can remember."

Facts Remembered	*Questions, if Needed*
Jim	(1. Who is it about?)
He studies the universe	(2. What does he do?)
That stars are suns	(3. What did he have trouble believing?)
That planets could be orbiting other suns (or stars)	(4. What did he figure out for himself?)

The child who develops the habit of recalling what he reads without prompting is likely to have better recall in all of his assigned reading. However, the child who must be prompted by a question for each item needs help. The teacher can develop paragraphs similar to the test items to give the child practice in recalling from short selections.

Since all the tests in this chapter are individual, the speed, volume, and clarity of the child's responses need to be noted along with their correctness. At the easy level of the test, how does the child show his comfort or enjoyment at succeeding; conversely, at the test ceiling, how does he show his frustration or discomfort?

The teacher who conscientiously collects this type of data is well on her way to applying continuous diagnosis. It is inconceivable that such a teacher would ever again listen to a group of children read without noting the position of errors, the types of errors, and other significant observations that are a part of a thorough evaluation.

4

DIAGNOSING POINTS OF ERROR

It is relevant to note that teachers' manuals, while helpful in avoiding some problems, cannot provide daily diagnoses and assistance. As a matter of fact, if the teacher is so bound to the teachers' manuals that she teaches a dozen or more words before the story is read, the child will have little opportunity to practice the skill of decoding new words in content. It is obviously impossible for the authors of teaching manuals to provide pertinent remedial ideas, since they have no way of knowing what specific errors different children will make.

One of the most important points to remember about a reading program is that it should include daily work-type and enjoyment-type reading. By "work type" we mean skill development, at whatever level needed: word-attack skills, content fluency, comprehension, or study skills.

Of equal, and in some cases more importance, is provision for enjoyment. Enjoyment reading is mainly at an independent level (which is usually half a grade below the child's instructional reading level). Here the pupil can apply the skills he has already learned. At this level, he reads without interruption. He needs the opportunity to discuss the content of this reading on a voluntary basis and in small groups. It is unwise to *test* the child on comprehension or expect analytical reports on this type of reading.

During instructional or work-type reading, the points of error may be diagnosed; however, even here the teacher refrains from interrupting the child's flow of thought. These levels of illustration follow: primary, intermediate, and upper grade:

Primary Level Work-Type Reading

The Child Knows:

> –the word *ride* in isolation as well as in a sentence; such as, I want to *ride* a bike.

Point of Error:

> However, when the child comes to the new word *wide* in a story he is reading (with minimal clues as to its meaning), as in–The street is *wide*–he is unable to generalize or reassemble known parts.

Procedure:

Give him one clue to the word. Think about his pattern of learning and give him a clue that is most appropriate for him. If he is quick to utilize meaning clues say, "What is the opposite of narrow?" If one clue is not sufficient, *tell him the word.* It is of utmost importance to know that reading conveys meaning, and that it is *not* laborious, *not* a time to review rules, and *not* a time to be interrupted by word-attack struggles. Note the point of his error, to be used at a later time as a basis for help–after the plot of the story has been understood, the paragraphs comprehended, and the sentences read.

Three possible clues to use are these:

> Clue 1–He knows "w" as a beginning sound.
> Clue 2–He knows "ide" as in *ride.*
> Clue 3–He knows *wide* is something a street can be.

If the child combines clues 1 and 3, there are many things he could think of that begin with "w" and fit in the sentence, such as–"A street is *wet, watered, wonderful, wanted,* and *washed-out.*" By attending to the first two clues, it is possible to blend the *w* and *ide* together to form the new word even though it was never seen before. The third clue, which is one of meaning, helps to check the correctness of the solution.

A common practice of teachers in dealing with failure to assemble known clues to form a new word is to present a list of new minimal pairs, such as the following:

bide hide
side wide

The teacher asks in what ways these words are alike and whether they remind the child of a known word. She can help refresh memories by writing the word *ride* on the board, if this is a word already known to the group. Most children will have no difficulty in noting that all the words are spelled with "ide" and rhyme with *ride*. If the letters *b, h, s,* and *w* are already known as initial consonants, the children should be able to sound out the new words–with a minimum of help.

This is fine as a first step, but in many cases, children need more help to transfer the new word into sentences! It is suggested that the teacher follow Step 1 by placing these words in simple sentences or having the children do this. The sentences can be as simple as the following:

1. *Bide* your time.
2. I can *hide* from you.
3. This *side* is up.
4. The box is *wide*.

In order to give the child practice in applying the skill that the teacher has just covered, she may save one word that fits the same pattern (for example, *tide*) and write this word in a simple sentence such as "The *tide* is high." The child will now have the opportunity to decode the new word in context. This provides a test of transfer of learning as well as valuable feedback. The process of transfer of learning is something that cannot be taken for granted. It is true that some children need no help because they will automatically blend known parts to form new words. They do this effortlessly because they have internalized the information. But other children need assistance through drills and games to practice the skills involved in blending known parts to form new words.

Related words can be changed by addition, subtraction, and substitution. The point of change can occur initially, finally, or medially. The key to reassembling word parts to form new words is that *meaning* should always be utilized whenever the new word appears in context. Whether the word is in isolation or in context, the following examples include common initial, final, and medial substitutions:

1. *Initial Substitutions*
   a. consonants: *t*urn, *b*urn
   b. consonant clusters: *dr*ag, *br*ag, *ch*urn
   c. vowels: *a*te, *e*at
   d. prefixes: *re*turn, *un*turn
2. *Final Substitutions*
   a. consonants: tur*n* - tur*f*, wi*n* - wi*t*
   b. consonant clusters: wi*th*, wi*sh*
   c. vowels: n*ow*, n*o*
   d. suffixes: wish*ing*, wish*ful*
3. *Medial Substitutions*
   a. consonants: lea*d*er, lea*p*er
   b. consonant clusters: chur*ch*less, mir*th*less
   c. vowels: c*a*t, c*o*t
   d. syllables: con*cer*ted, con*ten*ted

Intermediate and Upper Grade Level Work-Type Reading

At third or fourth grade, the children are apt to make syllable errors of substitution or omission.

The Child Knows:

> –the words *responsible* and *ability* in isolation or in content.

Point of Error:

> However, when the child comes to the sentence–The responsibility was too great for the boy–he substitutes *responsibly*, a four-syllable word for *responsibility* which is a six-syllable word.

Clue 1–He knows *responsi* as the correct first three syllables.
Clue 2–He correctly sounds the *y* vowel ending; he missed the medial and end syllables of *bil i ty*.
Clue 3–He knows *responsibility* is something that can be too great for a boy.

In this instance, it is likely that *responsibility* is not a word in the child's speaking vocabulary. Since if it were, the word two-thirds correctly pronounced would have triggered the correct response. Therefore, it will not be of any further help to give an additional clue; *tell him* the word. In doing so, you will give him a chance to respond to the sentence as a whole. Later you can give the student practice on words containing the same three syllables that were missed, such as: a*bility*, capa*bility*, reada*bility*, and desira*bility*. Save a word which fits the same pattern such as *usability* and put it in a sentence: "The pencil was so worn down, its *usability* was almost gone." This will give you a chance to see if the sound pattern transfers to a new word.

He also needs to know some meaning boundaries. One of the best ways to do this is to have children use the words in sentences and check with more than one dictionary.

So far we have been speaking about diagnosis on a daily basis, which is the best and most pertinent kind. On the other hand, it is possible to set up remedial lessons as a result of a test given without actually teaching the test words. For example, without teaching the identical word form, in some instances, you may teach the root word if the test word has an inflected ending. However, if the word missed in the test is a high-frequency word like *was* and is needed in daily reading, it obviously must be taught. The following report lists the word substitutions of an upper-grade boy, the point of error, and the words that could be used remedially to help the transfer of learning to words of similar patterns. These examples of errors are taken from a WRAT Reading Test, Level II.

WORD SUBSTITUTIONS	*POINTS OF ERROR*
*sp*it for *spl*it	1. sp for spl
*st*itch for *str*etch	2. *st* for *str*
	3. *itch* for *etch*
*thor*y for *theor*y	4. *thor* for *theor*, as in *the*orize
con*scious* for con*tagious*	5. two syllables for three syllables–*con ta gious* as in *cou ra geous*
grī*ve* for gr*ieve*	6. *ieve* as in bel*ieve* or retr*ieve*
tough for tough*en*	7. one syllable for two syllables–*en* ending as in rough*en*

board for *a*board	8. one syllable for two syllables–*a* prefix as in *a*round, *a*cross
*trĭ*mph for *trī*umph	9. one syllable for two syllables–*tri* as in *tri*pod
contem*pry* for contem*porary*	10. three syllables for five syllables, as in hon *or ar y*
es*cap* for es*cape*	11. *cap* for *cape*–e at the end of one syllable

The preceding error analysis is taken from the June report of a sixth-grade boy. Before suggesting remediation, it is advisable to have additional information about this student.

Student: William S. Actual Grade: *6-10*

William is a sophisticated, tall, good-looking, 12-year-old boy. He has to report to the principal's office a couple of times a month because, in his terminology, he "bugs" the teachers.

William's reading level is grade three; therefore, it is not surprising that he has never read a book of his own volition.

WISC	*Verbal*	118	*Performance*	112	*Total*	116
WRAT	*Reading*	3.5	*Spelling*	2.2	*Arith.*	5.7

Points of Error	*Errors and Suggestions*
Beginnings	
1. spit for *spl*it	The point of error is the beginning consonant cluster *spl*. Words that can be used which begin in this way are *splint, splinter.* (These words are better to use than *splash* because they not only have the same consonant cluster, but also the same short vowel.)
2. stitch for *str*etch	In substituting st for str, similar words such as *stress* and *strength* can be

used. Since these words both use the short *e*, they are better words to use than *strap* or *strong*.

3. board for *a*board

   The prefix *a* was ignored, so teach words such as *around* and *across*. Another point of error was the substitution of a single syllable for a two-syllable word.

4. trǐmph for *trī*umph

   The prefix *tri* has been missed. The word that can be used to correct this may be *tripod*. Another point of error was the substitution of a single syllable for a two-syllable word–and *tripod* will handle this also.

Medial Errors

1. conscious for con/*ta*/*gious*

   The middle syllable was missed entirely. The drill word to be used can be *contagion.* (Substitution of a two-syllable word for a three-syllable word.)

2. gr*īve* for gr*ieve*

   Long *ī* for the long *ē* medial sound. Words with a similar pattern–*ieve*–are *believe* and *retrieve.*

3. thory for the/o/*ry*

   Substitution of a two-syllable word for a three-syllable word. Use a word such as *theorize*, which has an identical middle syllable.

Endings

1. tough for tough*en*

   Since the error occurs by omitting the last syllable, we have selected *roughen* which has an identical last syllable.

2. contempry for contem/*po*/*rar*/*y*	Since the error occurs in the last syllables, the teacher can use words such as: *temporary, temporal,* or *temporize.* All of these words have a syllable identical with the one missed.
3. escap for *escape*	In this instance, it is desirable to list as many words as possible with short *a* which can be changed to long *a*, such as: cap - cape, tap - tape, rat - rate, fat - fate, rather than using vowels other than *a.*

Résumé on William

William is mature and socially secure enough to be told precisely how he scores. If on words in isolation he scores five months through the third grade, chances are good that he will score higher on reading in content. He is also intelligent enough to be taken into the confidence of the teacher in discussing his chances of succeeding. It should be explained to him that as he tries to analyze his own weaknesses and correct them (rather than wait for others to do this for him), he increases his own chance for success. He should be complimented for having only one initial consonant cluster error.

An error analysis follow-up takes items similar to the ones that were missed on the test and asks the child to pronounce them. The teacher then pronounces the word and asks the child if he can discover his point of error. For example, William said *spit* for *split* in the test. A similar item for the teacher to use with him, then, could be *splint*. If the child makes the same kind of error–*spint* for *splint*–it will be easy to see that the error occurs in the beginning of the word, in the consonant cluster *spl*. If one word is not sufficient to determine the error pattern, the teacher should employ two or three additional words.

Whenever the teacher selects words missed by the child, she should try to pick an example as similar as possible to the problem word–even if she uses the same root word, as can be noted in a few of the cases cited previously.

Children learn to analyze basic reading skills and comprehend in depth as they are encouraged to make up their own test items. This can be done by duplicating a nonscorable example from a standardized test to be worked through in class and then making up a similar item as a class project. With the completion of these two tasks, most of the children should be able to make up an item of their own to be worked out by a classmate. The children having difficulty with this task can be helped individually, by the teacher or a child who has already completed the task. Children who have the experience of creating and scoring original test items appear to develop a sophistication far superior to students without this experience. Figure 4-1 contains the test items made by children in an ungraded primary class.

After the child has been made aware of the point of error and has practiced other similar words, he should be helped to use these words in phrases and sentences. The child needs to practice applying the correct pronunciation of these words in short sentences.

All teachers need to be resourceful in finding words that fit the same pattern. Experienced teachers have often accumulated helpful lists of words that are readily accessible when needed, and to which new material is constantly being added. They are usually not only willing to share their material with new teachers, but also are quite eager to offer advice and tips from their own rich experiences. New teachers will find that an interchange of ideas and methods can be profitable and interesting. They will also find many other sources of help open to them. There are several books of particular value to beginning teachers: Anna Gillingham's *Remedial Training for Children with Specific Disabilities*[1] is very good. Selma Herr's[2] books on phonics are helpful, and in fact, most of the books on this area have much of interest to offer those engaged in teaching reading. Stott's[3] material from England has some very useful lists and activities. These are but a few of the many excellent aids which teachers may want to use as references in becoming familiar with words that fit certain

[1] Anna Gillingham, *Remedial Training for Children with Specific Disabilities in Reading, Spelling, and Penmanship* (Cambridge, Mass.: Educators Publishing Service, 1960).

[2] Selma Herr, *Phonics: Handbook for Teachers* (Los Angeles: E.R.A. Publishers, 1961).

[3] D. H. Stott, *Programmed Reading Kit* (Glasgow, Scotland: W. and R. Holmes, Ltd., n.d.).

Draw a line under ~~to~~ the tulip and to the girl.

Put a line under the painting.

2. 81 31 100 2000.

Put a line around the biggest number.

Figure 4-1

patterns. In the classroom, the most valuable resource is a well-trained, interested, and enthusiastic teacher, one who will use every possible device and technique to reach each child.

5

RECORD KEEPING AND CONFERENCING

From the moment the child first meets the teacher, a communication system is established. This may be the start of a very warm and helpful relationship, or the beginning of a reserved and tenuous one. At the outset, the child looks to the teacher for leadership and direction. In a desirable situation the teacher attempts to meet the expectations of the child, and in doing this she works with each child in a slightly different way. Even in the first days of school this means that to some children she provides support and to others opportunities for independent action. The most inadequate teacher would be the one who treats all children in the same way, demanding that the same amount of work be completed in the same length of time, and with the same degree of independence.

Dealing with the variety of individual differences found in present-day classrooms involves a multiplicity of tasks and problems that must be met by the modern, progressive teacher. While she realizes this and is eager to use every means at her command to bring each child to his potential, it is frequently difficult to implement a program that will do this. Record keeping is probably one of the greatest problems for a teacher seeking to individualize instruction, yet detailed records are of great importance in this type of program. Because the teacher has different expectations for each child in accordance with his capacity, attitude, and present level of performance, she must initiate a system of record keeping appropriate for the task, yet not so time-consuming as to cause her to abandon the whole program.

Each teacher will need to set up her own system. It is suggested that two types of records be kept–one, a detailed account which could be kept by the child, and the other, a more general appraisal by the teacher. For the teacher who has never kept records of this kind, and who does not have access to any previous system, a sample is given here that may be of some assistance. This record-keeping form, devised for use with an average public school class, can easily be adapted for any group.

One system of assessing a child's level of learning is through sensory involvement, matching, elaborating, locating, decoding, and automatically responding (SMELDA).

The six articulated levels are:

S - Sensory Involvement

a. forming as in clay
b. three-dimensional manipulating, feeling
c. tracing

M - Matching

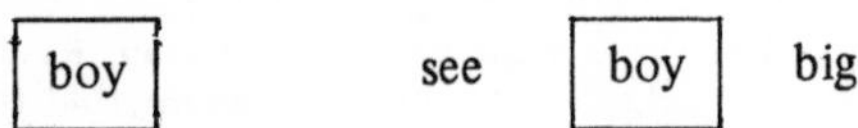

E - Elaborating

a. on external configuration
b. on internal configuration
c. number of ascending and descending letters
d. length

L - Locating

"Which word is boy?"

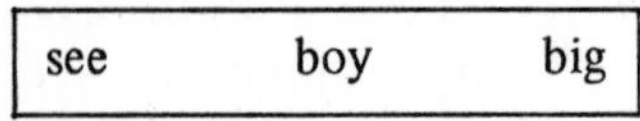

D - Decoding

a. recognizing similar parts
b. matching the written word to one already known in speech
c. sounding out a word not yet known in speech

A - Automatic Response

immediate, effortless, and accurate response

Rarely is it necessary to provide instruction for all six steps. The child who already *matches* identical words with ease does not need to be given sensory involvement. The child who can *locate* words as he hears them pronounced is already beyond the need of elaborating on word forms. Finally, the child who gives an *automatic* response to the stimulus word is already past the deliberate sounding out or thinking through of words in a decoding process. Since the average child does not require all six steps, our record keeping is limited to the three crucial milestones in word identification: matching, locating, and responding automatically.

Annual record sheets are duplicated for the teacher's use in noting the child's progress in sight vocabulary and in word-attack skills. The charts are marked on skill in matching, locating, and automatically responding as follows: a horizontal line — indicating ability to match; a vertical line | indicating ability to locate a letter or word from others in a list.

The lowest level of awareness is the matching level. An example of the ability to match and the ability to locate follows:

Checkup on Matching and Locating Ability

MATCHING LEVEL "—"

Teacher: "Look at the word in the box. Find and circle the word that looks most like it from the three words at the right."	and	an	Dan	and

(The next level is to locate the word as one of three printed words, after hearing rather than seeing the word.)

LOCATING LEVEL " | "

Teacher: "Circle the word *can*."	can	come	and

Groups of children can be tested to see whether they can match or locate the letter or word correctly. If the students are capable of automatically recalling the information, it is not necessary to begin at the level of matching or locating. Place an "X" on the square if the child can automatically recall or *read* the words he has correctly located. (This step should be checked on a one-to-one basis.)

Sheet I contains words which must be known by the child *before* he is given a preprimer. The child will have practiced the words in his personal writing, will have been tested on them, and consequently, will know them when he reads them in a printed book. Therefore, the words that appear on Sheet I must be taken from whatever basal or trade book the child will be reading. The words we have included in the example are from the Harper & Row preprimer, *Janet and Mark.*[1]

SIGHT VOCABULARY
SHEET I
Harper & Row–*Janet and Mark*

	(animals and people) I, Janet, Mark, Socks	(numbers) one, two, three	(action words) go, can, jump, ride, see, come	(places) up, down, here, in	(service words) the, my, and
Mary A.	⊠	⊠	⊠	⊠	⊠
John B.	—	—	—		
Annette B.	⊠	⊠	⊠	—	—

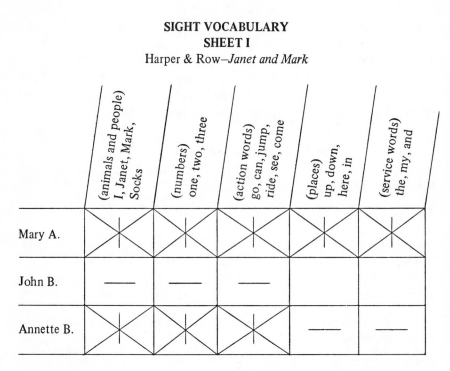

The third level of automatic recall should be checked on a one-to-one basis. In other words, the child reads to the teacher all of the words he recognizes at the locating level.

At a glance, the teacher can see that Mary A. is ready to read *Janet and Mark.* Quick access to pertinent information is a further advantage of such records.

No child is allowed to bungle through the first book he is given to read. Instead, his first experience offers an opportunity to show off–by reading words with which he is already thoroughly familiar.

---

[1] Mabel O'Donnell, *Janet and Mark* (New York: Harper & Row, 1966).

For example, Mary A. has read: | Mary can ride. | | John can jump. | | Annette can jump down. | She and others acted out and drew what they read. Mary A. discovered that most of these same experiences were similar to those in *Janet and Mark*.

If a basal series is used, a sight vocabulary sheet should be kept for *each* reader at least through Grade 3. In instances in which the publishers include vocabulary tests, part of the teacher's work is already done. The tabulation sheets for recording information are the responsibility of the teacher.

SHEET A – PHONICS

Color Code:
Sept.-Nov. – black
Dec.-Feb. – green
March-May – red

Initial Consonants
Short Vowels
Digraphs
Initial Consonant Clusters

CHILD'S NAME		*b c f h t*	*a e i o u*	*p m j k s*	*d l g r w*	*z y qu n v*	*wh sh ch th*	*bl cl fl gl pl sl*	*br cr fr gr pr tr*
	KEY WORDS	bat cat fat hat tat	bat bet bit bot but	pumps mumps jumps kit sit	dig lag gig rig wig	zip yip quip nip van	whip ship chip that	blot clot flat glad plot slot	brag crack from grit prim trim
Mary A.		X	X	X	X	X	X	X	X
John B.		—	—						
Annette B.		X	X	X					

In addition to the records kept on basal vocabulary, it is helpful to keep records on the child's knowledge of phonics. It is important that the phonics record sheets be dovetailed to fit the reading program in the classroom. Phonics Sheet A, which covers initial consonants, short vowel sounds, initial consonant digraphs, initial consonant clusters, and which uses monosyllables as key words, is included here as an example.

Automatic recall on the phonics sheets differs from automatic recall on the sight vocabulary sheets. You will observe that on the phonics sheets, automatic recall refers to filling in the missing phonics elements; while on the vocabulary sheets, it means reading the word. An example is included to demonstrate the difference.

AUTOMATIC RECALL

Teacher: "Write in the first two letters of the word *from*."	1. _ _ o m.
"Write in the first two letters of the word *crack*."	2. _ _ a c k.

Since we can teach children how to facilitate transfer of learning, it is not necessary to cover *all* consonant clusters, prefixes, suffixes, or root words. The sample words used in *Sheet D* are enough to convey the idea that root words and affixes carry meaning. As root words and affixes with known meanings are combined, the new words formed can be figured out by the student.

Children can be made to feel that they are partners in the business of keeping records, and this tends to develop in them a feeling of importance. For this purpose, each child needs a loose-leaf notebook or file folder divided into two parts. One of the sections will contain skill sheets that have been duplicated by the teacher, and the other part will contain blank sheets on which the child keeps a log (this can be done by all grades but the first). The following will give an idea of the type of information that could be kept by each child (page 91).

The log kept by the student constitutes a personal account of what he considers important to him each day. It is not necessarily written in sentences, but rather in a style or code understood by the writer. This account is not to be considered a diary in the sense that it is a record of each day's happenings for private perusal only, but it is a personal record in that the child may employ his own means of

MY NAME IS ______________________________

____

1. I know the names of the letters that I have circled:

   A B C D E F G H I J K L M N
   O P Q R S T U V W X Y Z

2. I know the beginning of the key words which I have circled:
   (consonants)

bat	pumps	dig	zip
cat	mumps	lag	yip
fat	jumps	gig	quip
hat	kit	rig	nip
tat	sit	wig	van

3. I know the beginnings of the words which I have circled:
   (consonant clusters)

*wh*ip	*b*lot	*g*lad	*b*rag	*g*rit
*sh*ip	*c*lot	*p*lot	*c*rack	*p*rim
*ch*ip	*f*lat	*s*lot	*f*rom	*t*rim
*th*at				

recording events. The daily account is not a lesson in spelling or usage, nor is it to be used as a class reading project. It is, however, strictly between the teacher and the child, and is subject to the teacher's reviewal at any time. It may provide her with helpful clues about the child.

The benefits derived from involving students in the task of record keeping are dual; the teacher is helped in keeping detailed and pertinent data and the child is able to note his daily progress.

REPORTING TO PARENTS

Conferences with parents can be pleasant as well as informative. Ordinarily, it is wise to begin the conference with the child present. Let the child demonstrate or share whatever he has learned by way of vocabulary development or reading skills. Help him to select what he does *well*. Approximately one-third of the conference time should include the child. After the child leaves, encourage the parents to share information. They may be invited to tell how they feel about their child and his reading. This gives them a chance to talk about one of their favorite subjects, and also gives them an opportunity to bring forth any grievances they might have.

Sheets B, C, and D list other word-attack skills that should be covered as follows:

SHEET B – PHONICS

Consonant Endings
Inflected Endings
Long Vowel Sounds

	b t p m k	s d l g r	z v n sh	ch th ng	s ed ing	ly ful fully	er	a e i o u
KEY WORDS	tab tat tap tam tack	kiss bed bell beg beggar	buzz love fin fish	catch with wing	helps helped helping	lovely helpful careful helpfully carefully	catcher buzzer fisher helper backer	cake Pete kite hope cute
NAMES								

Parents are then ready to listen to a specific reading report describing the various goals set for the class and the methods used to attain them. The child's own growth is considered as a self-competitive record. While it is unfair to compare individual children, it is *not* unfair to compare an individual's record with the average record of the group in which he is working. This gives a parent an idea of the frustrations the child may feel if his performance falls short of the group average.

Most parents are singularly impressed by the completeness of the teacher's records on their child. They appreciate hearing about the specific skills that are covered. You may have observed that at no

SHEET C – WORD-ATTACK SKILLS
Small Letter

c → k, s

Compound words
vc/cv
v/cv
/c le

	y = ī	y = ē	c = s	c = k	compound words	vc/cv	v/cv	/c le
KEY WORDS	cry	lady	city	cat	doghouse	dentist	obey	able
	dry	Tommy	cent	cot	lookout	pencil	silent	cradle
	fry	kindly	citizen	cut	seesaw	walnut	divide	table
	pry	windy	certain	clash	boxcar	swallow	travel	marble
	try	city		crash	cowboy	mustard	minus	stable
	wry	busy			newsboy	doctor	gravy	purple
NAMES								

time have we mentioned *grades* as used in traditional reporting. The goals in a reading program consist of *levels* of performance in oral and silent reading, and these are the only specifics worth reporting. Grades have been palliative in the past. A system which provides the teacher with complete records of the child's individual achievements has no need to pigeonhole the child into one of the traditional grading categories–particularly since one of these classifications is failure. Glasser states this case well in *Schools Without Failure.*[2]

---

[2] William Glasser, *Schools Without Failure* (New York: Harper & Row, 1969).

SHEET D – WORD-ATTACK SKILLS

Root words
Prefixes
Suffixes

	aqua water, liquid	*phon phone* sound, voice, speech, tone	*graph* writing, or instrument for transmitting	*ab* from	*re* back, again	*er or* one who	*ment* act of
KEY WORDS	aqua-phone aquar-ium aque-duct	phone pho-netic phono-graph	graph graph-ite auto-graph	abduct ab-normal ab-sence	re-buff recur re-count	catch-er batter doc-tor	govern-ment develop-ment move-ment
NAMES							

Toward the close of the conference, it is desirable to summarize the child's achievements and strengths, enumerate new goals to be attained, and advise parents on the best methods of supplementing the school's reading program. Some of the usual suggestions made to parents are:

–to provide time and access to library and reference books.
–to read about a place before traveling to it.
–to provide a comfortable area for reading in the home.
–to discuss books and articles as a family activity.

Occasionally, some parents will exert too much pressure on a child. When this is noted, it is wise to persuade them to relax and trust the school to handle the reading program.

Conferences should be set up at the convenience of all concerned. First, parents should be invited in small groups to observe their child in reading activities. Ordinarily, the teacher finds it expedient to schedule conferences with gifted children and their parents early in the year. These children are readily identified, as they accomplish goals easily and are eager to move on to the next task. Conferences concerning average children usually follow those of the gifted group. These, too, are fairly easy to conduct because there are more positive then negative points to discuss. Conferences with parents of slow-performing children, while positive in tenor, may be difficult to conduct because parents are often unable to adjust to having a slow-paced child in the family. By placing these conferences last, the teacher has the opportunity to discover the child's strengths and gather more information as to how the parent can reinforce the reading program. These conferences will require a great deal of preparation and tact. In planning for them, it is imperative that the teacher discover some particular talent or strength that the child may possess. This may be in any field, and in any degree, and might take the form of skill in some type of dancing, physical prowess on the playground, talent in singing, or facility in mimicry. By incorporating in the conference some discussion of a child's talent or strength, the teacher may establish rapport with the parents. They may well realize that the teacher and the school are as interested in the welfare of their child as they are.

In summary, the "in" group—that is, the child, the teacher, and the parents—are most directly concerned with the quality of teaching, objectives, and methods. Those points of communication and interest that are effective at the "in" group level will also spill over to the "outer" group or the surrounding community. The smooth dialogue thus established creates limitless horizons that *start* at the door of the classroom instead of ending there. The more channels of communication that can be kept open, the freer the flow of information to the public. The more the public knows of what is being done in the classroom, the more faith they will have in what can be done for *all* children.

PART II

TEACHING FOR INDEPENDENCE

6

BUILDING FLUID READERS

In fluid oral reading, speech flows with a richness that brings life to the printed word. Even ancient tomes come alive when read with fluidity.

This chapter is concerned with the need for building fluid oral readers as a basis for the development of efficient silent readers. Fluid readers have some common attributes. They can quickly identify known words, rapidly figure out new words from sound, sense, and structure clues, and interpret the author's intent with ease. The students who become masters of the printed page are likely to enjoy the power they possess. Their enjoyment leads to more reading and even greater power, ***ad infinitum.***

Until the day we step into our monorail and press a dot on a map as our destination, and order food from televised intercom, we will continue to be classed as a reading society. Oral reading economically gives the teacher an opportunity for continuous diagnosis. However, if oral reading is accurate but colorless and even odious, chances that the student will become an effective silent reader are remote. We tend to pursue activities which are both successful and enjoyable.

FLUID READERS

Oral readers become successful fluid readers because they can rapidly identify words and briefly hold them in mind to be used as needed. The difference in the eye-voice span is the length of time that a word needs to be held in mind. To measure the eye-voice span, have the pupil read aloud from an easy story. Then suddenly cover the line from which he is reading with an index card. The number of words he continues to read after the line is covered is his eye-voice span. The pupil who stops reading as soon as the card covers the line is a word-by-word reader. He needs to be taught to look ahead to facilitate the flow of words.

Some children develop this fluidity naturally from the example of fluid readers around them, while other children need to have the steps set up for them. The following are suggestions structured to increase the accuracy of the beginning reader. Use them if they fit the needs of your students.

First we suggest matching activities, but these are to be below the level of naming or reading. For instance, the child can see the word *happy* and match it with its meaning without being able to name or read the word. Choose words which are meaningful to him, such as his name and other children's names. Words may also be selected which he will eventually be reading, such as the words from the first preprimer. These words will become familiar to the child through repetition in the matching activities. These words will be easy to match before any pressure is felt by the child to read them. The child who is already reading should not be included in these activities.

The following word-matching activities are appropriate for those children who are past the letter-matching stage but who cannot read any words other than their own names. It is recommended that the teacher have no more than six children in a group. As the children learn how these activities are conducted, they can participate in small groups with a child in the role of teacher.

Material: Make two sets of preprimer word cards–one set of 32 colored word cards for children and one set in white of 32 word cards for the teacher. These cards are used in all the activities described. An example taken from Lyons and Carnahan[1] 1972 follows:

Example:

a	happy	is	Mom
be	he	let	my
can	here	like	no
can't	I	little	not

[1] Margaret LaPray and Ramon Ross, *Little Pig* (Chicago: Lyons & Carnahan, 1972).

go	in	me	oh
out	play	stay	will
pig	school	stays	with
pigs	see	to	you

Word-Matching Activity No. 1–LOOK-ALIKES

1. Teacher selects a one-letter white word card to place face up in the wall chart.
2. Each child in turn draws a colored word card, which he keeps face down until everyone has a card.
3. Teacher says, "Now, look at your word." Everyone looks to see if their card matches the card in the wall chart.
4. If no one turned over a card that matched, each person returns the card to the bottom of the deck and draws another one.
5. As soon as one child has picked the right card, it is placed on the wall chart so everyone in the group may compare the two.
6. If the card is correct, the child who found it is now the teacher. He then looks for any word in the white deck that has *two* letters. Continue to play in the same way. Each new word selected adds one additional letter. The wall chart could look like this after four turns.

I		I
to		to
let		let
like		like

Word-Matching Activity No. 2–MORE OR LESS

1. The teacher holds up a long word, such as the name of a state or the name of the child's own school: Washington.
2. She asks one child at a time if his name is longer or shorter.
3. The teacher should select words that differ greatly in length such as:

   [I] [California].

4. As the children develop a finer discrimination, words closer in length can be used.
5. After the children understand what is expected of them, stick to the preprimer words.

Word-Matching Activity No. 3–MATCH BEGINNINGS

(Special letter cards for the teacher [c] [h] [i] [l] [m] [p] [s] [w] [n])

1. Pass out a colored word card to each child.
2. Teacher places a letter card in the wall chart. The children who have words that begin with this letter place their cards in the wall chart and draw another card from the deck.
3. The letter cards remain on display.
4. Every time the child places a card in the chart, he gets one point.

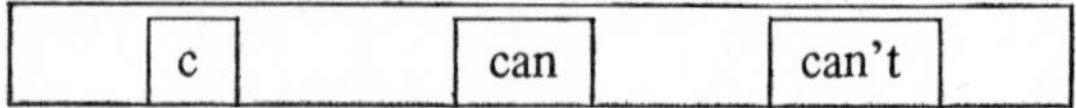

Word-Matching Activity No. 4–DESCRIBE IT

1. One child is chosen to stand up front by the teacher.
2. All of the other children are given colored cards, which they study and then hold up toward the teacher and the chosen child to see.
3. The chosen child looks at all of the cards. She selects and describes one of the words: "It has four letters–two of the letters are tall and two of the letters are half size."

4. As soon as the child whose card is described recognizes it, he can be the next one chosen. Otherwise, whichever child recognizes the card first becomes the chosen one.

Word-Matching Activity No. 5–SAMPLE CONCENTRATION

1. Show the children four white word cards.
2. Hold up one at a time and say, "Look carefully. Watch where I put this. Try to remember where it is." Then place the card face down any place in the pocket chart–continue until all four cards are placed.
3. Then pass out the four colored cards that match the face-down cards. (If there are eight children in the group, have one card for each two children.)
4. As soon as two children can successfully locate the cards that match, they win.
5. If they are wrong, they return the original white card face down again. The object is to have all the cards correctly matched.

Word-Matching Activity No. 6–FLOOR CONCENTRATION

1. The teacher selects *n* number of matched pairs (identical words).
2. The children watch as each of the matched pairs is placed face down.
3. A child picks up one of the cards.
4. He tries to remember where the mate to that card is.
5. If he succeeds, he gets two points and the next child gets a turn.
6. If he does not find a mate, he must show the rest of the group exactly where he replaces his card face down.

Word-Matching Activity No. 7–SIZE THIS UP

1. The teacher puts four cards face up in the wall chart.
2. She writes one of these words in a huge size (probably on the board).
3. She asks the class to see how quickly they can find a similar card from the wall chart (in spite of the difference in size).
4. She may write one of the words in miniature.
5. The class members see how quickly they can find a similar card.
6. The teacher continues to vary the sizes and observe how quickly they can find a similar card.

Word-Matching Activity No. 8–RACE ME

1. Teacher puts four, six, or eight cards face up in the wall chart (four for immature groups, eight for mature groups).
2. "Watch as I start to write one of these words. As soon as you know which word it could be, raise your hand."
3. She stops after putting the first letter on the board.
4. Accept any card beginning with this letter.
5. Copy the complete card.
6. Keep score for the girls and boys if you consider this appropriate.

Word-Matching Activity No. 9–MIND READING

1. The teacher gives all but one child a colored card.
2. The child without a card leaves the room.
3. While he is gone, the teacher copies the letters of a word on the board. After everyone has seen the word, it is erased.
4. The child who was excluded is called back to the room.
5. He guesses which one of the children's cards contains what the teacher had written on the board.
6. The class tells him when he guesses correctly. The emphasis in this activity is on the ability of the class to hold a word in their own minds.

Word-Matching Activity No. 10–FIND AND MATCH

1. The teacher puts a card from the colored set face down in front of each child.
2. She says, "Close your eyes."
3. Then she hides the matching cards from the white set in various places around the room.
4. "Open your eyes. Find the card that matches your card. It is someplace in this room."
5. In this game, encourage the children to help one another.

(At Easter time it's fun to paste colored eggs over the backs of the cards.)

The preceding ten activities can be adapted to suit the needs of your group. Continue to use only the learning activities that are enjoyed by your children. Additional ways to prepare a child for reading are published by Houghton Mifflin Co.[2] in a booklet originally prepared for parents but which is equally helpful for teachers.

For the beginning reader, there is some merit in having the child tell the teacher the word he is interested in learning as suggested by Grace Fernald[3] and Sylvia Ashton-Warner.[4] The words selected without any controls, as in the two references given, are most feasible in a tutorial situation.

COMMON WORD SOURCE

Another method which is more appropriate for classroom use is to have the child select words from a common source, such as a story or poem. For example, the teacher reads a poem such as the following:

Spaceboy

Quite a sight, one night!
A wee boy, a big kite.
As gusty winds blew,
His problems grew.
With fists held tight–
He launched into flight–
"Look, a wee satellite."

The first time the teacher reads the poem, she asks the children to close their eyes and see if they can picture the size of the boy and the kite, and what happens to them. For the second reading, she has each line of the poem placed on a sentence strip. This time the teacher puts the strip in the pocket chart as she reads it aloud. She has the end word of each line already printed in red on flash cards. Then she says, "See if you can figure out what I am doing." She carefully places the flash card for [night] over the end word in line one; the word [kite] over the end word in line two; and the rest of the flash cards over each one of the end words in the remaining lines.

---

[2] Joseph Brezeinski and Bertha Stevens, *Preparing Your Child for Reading* (Boston: Houghton Mifflin, 1961).

[3] Grace M. Fernald, *Remedial Techniques in Basic School Subjects* (New York: McGraw-Hill, 1966).

[4] Sylvia Ashton-Warner, *Teacher* (New York: Simon & Schuster, 1963).

As soon as the children have figured out that all of the flash cards have words identical to the ones at the end of the line, she can continue:

Teacher says:	*Child says:*
"I will read the lines, again. This time whoever says the last word of the line first can come up and get the flash card with the word on it." (Each child is allowed only one word.)	
Quite a sight, one	night
A wee boy, a big	kite etc.

It is very likely that satellite will be the most popular word. Give the children a chance to exchange words as soon as they have learned them. Next, the teacher can put the sentence strips out of order on the floor. Have the children select the strips to be placed in the chart in order. Later on, let the children choose the last two or three words that appear on the strip: *one night, a big kite, winds blew, problems grew, held tight, into flight,* and *a wee satellite.* Then in choral reading fashion, the teacher reads the first part of the line and the students read the last part. At subsequent meetings, you may have a precocious child who wants to read the part that the teacher reads. This is fine. The secret of being successful in teaching from a controlled selection of words is giving words only to the child who wants them, and allowing enough time to hold, to study, and to use them. The method described involves a common core from which to select and several chances to read a word as part of a total performance. The technique of having children select a word on their own from a common source is also classed as aural-oral reading. That is, the teacher always reads the selection several times so that the children hear a good oral pattern before they are expected to participate in producing one. Additional suggestions for developing aural-oral techniques can be found in the teachers' manuals of the books edited by Bill Martin, *Sounds of Language.*[5]

Words are selected to be taught, first of all, because they will be of immediate use in a reading selection, and, secondly, because they fit similar sound or structure patterns. Teachers' manuals that accom-

[5] Bill Martin, Jr., *Sounds of Language Readers* (New York: Holt, Rinehart & Winston, 1966).

pany basal reading series include sections to develop both of these competencies. The teacher can adapt these suggestions by personalizing the exercises.

If the three words to be introduced in the story are *which, boy,* and *fast*, she can relate these words to the children in her class:

Which boys can run *fast?*

Bill is *fast.*

John is *fast*, etc.

Which girls can run *fast?*

Ann is *fast*, etc.

She can relate the sound and structure to names and events common to the children in the classroom, such as:

- *Which* rhymes with *Petrowich* and *sandwich*.
- *Boy* rhymes with *toy, joy*, and *coy*—as Jeanne is *coy*.
- *Fast* rhymes with *cast*—like the *cast* Joe had on his leg.
- *Mast* is like the *mast* Bill had on his toy sailboat.

COMMERCIAL READING

Frequently the teacher prepares pupils to read from books, magazines, or newspapers. One successful way to do this is to use words and phrases taken from the selection and personalize them. To illustrate how this could be done, we have included the following dialogue which two boys in the class will be expected to read:

"It's so black out tonight, I can't see my hand in front of my face," Joe said.

"I know it." Bob shivered a little.

"Do you think we're safe in this little tent?" said Joe.

"We do have a flashlight," Bob said, as he turned on a weak light.

"Turn it off. We've got to save it."

Before the teacher introduces this magazine selection, she prepares to use as many of the words and phrases as she can, but in a personal context.

If the boys in the group have camped, the teacher can draw on this experience. If not, she can ask them to pretend they are camping.

Next, the teacher feeds in the events that occur in the magazine selection and asks which boy thinks he might say that. The teacher says, "It's dark on the campground, but in the tent it's black." Which one of you might have said, "It's so black out tonight?" Chris volunteers. The teacher writes the quotation on a card followed by *said Chris*. She then gives the card to Chris to read with as much expression of fear as he can. In a similar manner, she assigns every quotation to a volunteer member of the group. After the boys have gained fluency with the made-up event, they are given the original magazine selection. The teacher asks if they notice any similarities. Usually they smile as they see that most of the quotations are the same.

Another way to prepare for an original selection is to pull out the phrases and use them in a different context. Using the same example as before, you could say, "Two children went out on Halloween night. It was black and spooky. When they got home_____."

Father said:	*The children said:*
What is it like outside?	so black out
Could you see your hand?	in front of my face
Was it so cold you __________	shivered a little
Were you out in the open or __________	in a little tent
What did you have for a light?	a flashlight
How did it light?	it turned on
What kind of a light did it give?	a weak light
What can be done to save the light?	turn it off
Why did you turn the flashlight off?	to save it

Review the phrases in the following ways:

1. Repeat what the father said–have the boys repeat what the children said.
2. The teacher reads what the children said–the boys race to find it on the board.
3. Have the boys read the phrases in the order in which they appear on the blackboard.
4. Have the children cover their eyes. Erase one of the phrases. See if they can remember the one erased.

5. Ditto "Phrase-O" cards with the phrases on them. Distribute them and have the children tear nine small pieces of paper ready for use.

turn it off	a weak light	
to save it		shivered a little
	it turned on	a flashlight

The children copy from the board the phrases that are left, placing them in any square they want to. As the teacher calls out a phrase, children recognizing it cover the appropriate square with a piece of paper. When three in a row are covered, the winner calls out "Phrase-O." If he is capable of doing so, he reads the phrases back. If he is not beyond the stage of recognition, the teacher will check the child's card for him.

After all of this preparation, the children can turn to the original selection with a comfortable feeling that words and phrases "are easy."

WORD FLIP STRIPS

Flip strips are an interesting way to teach the words of a song. The technique provides for plenty of time to identify each word and staple them in sequence. The second step allows practice in reading the lines of a song, and the last step is a group performance. Note the following:

On 1.	I 3.	It 5.	It 7.
top	lost	bounced	splattered
of	my poor	on	the
spaghetti	meatball	the table	carpet

All 2.	When 4.	It 6.	And 8.
covered	some	fell	rolled
with	body	on	out
cheese	sneezed	the floor	the door

The words of this song are printed on sheets of 8½ X 11 inch paper, each of which has been divided into 16 equal strips (four boxes of four strips). On each strip will appear one word or phrase from the song, and the first strip of each box will have a number: 1, 2, 3, 4, 5, 6, 7, or 8 (so that the children are aided in assembling each of the eight lines of the song).

These two sheets are to be duplicated and handed to each child for cutting and assembling the strips. Using the tune of "On Top of Old Smokey," sing the following song–line-by-line:

On top of spaghetti
All covered with cheese,
I lost my poor meatball,
When somebody sneezed.
It bounced on the table,
It fell on the floor.
It splattered the carpet,
And rolled out the door.

Start with two children. Say, "See how quickly you can find the words I just sang from Box 1. Cut and put them in order, the first word on top, the second word next, the third word next, and the fourth word on the bottom. Staple the left end of the packet so that you can flip over the strips and read them to me."

Proceed in a similar manner, line-by-line, through the rest of the song. To make this a continuous teaching situation, have the two pupils who finished their flip strips each choose another child to show how the activity is done. The pupils do not have to know the word *spaghetti* in order to choose the word correctly. They need only to know that *spaghetti* begins with *s*. No other word in that line begins with *s*.

See if the students can flip over each strip as you sing, one line at a time. Since most strips have one word only, this takes some fast flipping.

Think of as many ways as possible to help your students learn these words; such as putting the lines in order, finding words that begin with *s*, or choose some other letter. Hum a line and see who can find and read the line you are humming; sing a line omitting a word and see who can find the word you omitted. You can enrich your sing-a-longs by bringing in a guitar, autoharp, or instrument of your choice.

Try some parodies. The first one you do with the class may take more teacher assistance than subsequent ones. The following example is a parody composed in class to be sung to the tune of "On Top of Old Smokey":

I saddled old Pokey,
My Palomino,
But he was so ancient,
That he wouldn't go.

I gave him a carrot,
And walloped his side,
As he got the message,
I flew far and wide!

One of the activities your class may enjoy with their new verse is to relay-read one word at a time in rapid sequence in a word-recognition race. Each student reads one word in turn. This is different from reading rapidly. No attempt should be made to have the child individually race through the entire verse. This is not a desirable goal—but it is desirable to recognize words immediately and enjoy doing so.

These are just a few ways to aim for a target of reading enjoyment. Like parts of a master jigsaw puzzle, the teacher builds with bits and pieces until the child puts together a colorful picture.

And there the analogy ends, because from words and phrases the picture gains life. The child sees, tastes, and smells; he loves and cries. What the author captured lies dormant on the page, until revived by the child.

7

REACTING TO CONTENT CLUES

All reading is reacting to content clues. It really doesn't matter whether the child is reacting to Social Studies or Henny Penny. What does matter is whether he has the technical and experiential background to respond readily to the content of whatever he reads.

His purpose for reading dictates the rate. He will rapidly scan the chapter if his purpose is to locate items as quickly as possible; he will lightly skim the chapter if his purpose is to comprehend as much as he can in a short period; and he will slowly savor the chapter if his purpose is to understand "meaty" content and intriguing style.

While all reading is reacting to content, there is a spectacular difference in most children's experiential background in literature and in specific subject areas. Their reading diet from ages 3 through 7 has been primarily stories and poems. Only rarely during these years is the reading made up of subject-matter articles. Today's first-grade child is much more apt to be exposed to Kipling's *How the Rhinoceros Got His Skin*[1] than to a factual account of how baby rhinos live. It is an integral part of our present culture that young children listen to and begin to read from stories and poems written primarily to entertain.

In addition to an early and pleasant association with literature, three more factors operate to assure a successful introduction to stories and poems. One of these factors is the availability of literary

[1] Rudyard Kipling, *Just So Stories* (Garden City, N. Y.: Doubleday, 1922).

selections in inexpensive editions. Similar enrichment is obtained through such well-researched TV programs, as the pioneer production in 1969 of "Sesame Street." Another strong factor is the child's common experiential background with the characters in the stories and poems, which produces empathy. The animals in these early books are anthropomorphic. Like a disobedient child, Peter Rabbit gets into trouble and is sent to bed without his supper. Another factor contributing to success is the teachers' manuals which accompany the basal readers, and which, in fact, give more help than most teachers need.

Children rarely have comparable experiences when subject matter is read to them. Parents seldom reward good behavior by reading science or mathematics to a child. Conceivably, some good could come from including such subjects as a more important part of early childhood experience. The value which adults place on the subject would then be transferred to the child, and at the same time, the child would be building up a backlog of useful information.

Interest in science, mathematics, and social studies can easily grow out of children's favorite stories. The Three Bears story can be employed to help children discover scientific facts. Even a fantasy such as this frequently contains some factual basis to make the story credible. Possible statements which could be discussed are:

1. Bears do live in the forest.
2. Bears can walk on their hind paws.
3. Mother, father, and baby bear might choose to go for a walk in the woods.
4. The bears were probably a species called "brown bears."
5. They live in northern Asia and Europe.
6. They can be tamed and trained to perform tricks.

Again, this same fanciful story can be used to pull out the concept of mathematical sets. There are some sets of one; i.e., the girl, the house, and the broken chair. There are sets of two—the two items that never suited. There are sets of three:

The child of a mathematician is apt to go far in deciding which sets are equivalent and which, if any, are equal. Other children will barely be able to comprehend the concept of three as being more than one and two. Yet regardless of these differences, by extending the child's knowledge, his readiness to comprehend mathematics is greater than it would otherwise have been.

Interest in science can develop from what the child sees happening around him. The preschool son of a zoology professor was surprised one morning to find that in the cage of his pet garden snake there were 18 tiny, squirming replicas of his pet. It was at this point in the boy's quest for knowledge that he wanted answers. A factual picture book would have filled a definite need in his life. It might also have awakened the excitement of finding answers "on his own."

In the example cited, the background of the boy is of the utmost importance. Under too much pressure, the child might well have learned to hate snakes—but in this case, he developed an interest in them. In other words, the key person to decide whether content is to be of interest or value is the child himself.

RECIPROCAL QUESTIONING

Although the key person is the child, there are some techniques that will help him to be a more effective reader. Reciprocal questioning is one of them. No matter what he reads, whether it be detective stories or a herpetologist's reference, he will be better attuned to the content if he develops a questioning attitude.

In reciprocal questioning at the sentence level, the child is first paired with the teacher. The questions may be complicated or simple, but they are not judged as being good or bad. In one instance, the child was so motivated by having the chance to question the teacher that he interrupted his recess time to tell her, "I just thought of another question." The following is a suggested procedure for reciprocal questioning (R/Q):

1. The child reads a sentence and thinks up a question.
2. He asks the teacher his question.
3. He waits for an immediate answer from the teacher.
4. He listens in turn to a question directed to him by the teacher.
5. He answers the teacher's question and directs a second question to the teacher.
6. He continues until there are no more questions to ask (or set a limit if you prefer).

The advantages of this technique are that the child must "zero in" on the content or he has no question to ask. He also experiences the satisfaction of having the partner's undivided attention in listening to him and in answering his questions.

To introduce the technique, the teacher should be one of the partners or she should have the technique demonstrated for the class members to observe. It is not unusual for the child to say he cannot think of a question, in which case, the teacher will have to supply the first question. In one week's time, by taking six children individually (three in the morning and three in the afternoon), she can introduce R/Q in from 5 to 10 minutes per child.

Minimum rules are as follows:

1. The questions emanate from the content.
2. Answers also emanate from the content.

Even a primary-level reader can learn the questioning process. The following is from a teacher-student reciprocal questioning period.

The sentence to be read is: The boy ran down the street.

Student: Who ran?

Teacher: *The boy*. Where did he run?

Student: *Down the street*. What did the boy do?

Teacher: *He ran*. Why did the boy run?

Student: (Tied to content–*It doesn't say*.) Usually people run because they are late or because they are afraid. What does *down* the street mean?

Teacher: It probably means he has not come to the end of the street yet or it could mean the street ran downhill. What punctuation mark follows *street*?

Student: A period. Who is important in this sentence?

Teacher: The *boy*. What is the first word in the sentence?

Student: *The*. Why is *the* capitalized?

Teacher: It is the first word in a sentence, and first words are always capitalized. Does any word appear more than once in this sentence?

Student: Yes, *the*. How can you change the sentence if the boy did not do what it said?

Teacher: The boy did not run down the street. What did I do to change this sentence?

Student: You made the sentence negative by changing the verb from ran to *did not run*. Which word tells you what action the boy took?

The object is not to evaluate the questions but to encourage a questioning attitude. Literal-level questions such as the following are likely to occur:

- Who ran?
- Where did he run?
- What did the boy do?

To recognize the literal meaning of the words in a sentence is a basic level of comprehension. It is the level of reading at which a technically correct pianist performs; whereas, a concert artist reads musical score at an interpretative level. Questions such as the following require interpretation:

- Why did the boy run?
- What does *down* the street mean?
- Who is important in this sentence? (The important person could have been interpreted as the one who *caused* the boy to run.)

Interpretative questions are answered in the light of the child's experiential background and, therefore, cannot be classed as right or wrong. They tell a great deal about the child's ability to deal with relationships, his environment, and his understanding of content. If the questioning is extensive, questions at the interpretative level are likely to occur naturally.

At the primary level, technical questions involving phonemes, morphemes, and syntax are also likely to occur. Questions dealing with transformations are apt to show up too (the following are technical questions):

- What punctuation follows street?
- What is the first word in the sentence?
- Why is *the* capitalized?
- Does any word appear more than once in this sentence?
- How would you change this sentence if the '*boy did not do what it said*'?
- What did I do to change this sentence?
- What word tells an action the boy took?

For upper-grade and secondary students, the procedure is the same. By using a more complicated statement the questions are likely to be more probing, as in the example that follows:

Immigration policies account for more of the population problem than the birthrate.

Student: What accounts for most of the population problem?

Teacher: The statement says that immigration policy does. Do you believe this?

Student: No. Because right now I don't know enough about it. Where could you collect data on this topic?

Teacher: From census reports and from population density maps. Do you think the birthrate is the biggest problem?

Student: According to Paul Ehrlich, it is. I haven't made up my mind yet. In what way do immigrants complicate the problem?

Teacher: They settle in the most densely populated areas and usually raise large families. Do the policies or the immigrants themselves contribute most to the population problem?

Student: I don't know what the present policies are so I can't answer that. Etc.

The distribution of questions among literal, interpretative, and technical levels varies with age groups. With the secondary student, you are likely to get only one or two questions at the literal level as in the preceding example. The four remaining questions in this example require interpretative or conjectural answers.

Students become involved and excited as they formulate their own questions. As they develop a questioning attitude toward all of the content, concentration becomes easier. The widespread use of teacher-guided questions and student-made study questions could both be strengthened, if not replaced, by the use of R/Q.

Reciprocal questioning (R/Q) at the sentence level is only the beginning of its application. The technique is equally effective at the paragraph, article, or story level.

After the student has developed some fluency at the sentence level, introduce the technique at the paragraph level. The following example is taken from a Social Studies lesson:

Brazilians, more than any people in Latin America except the Mexicans, have analyzed their own national characteristics frankly. One writer has drawn up a list of '27 Unfavorable Realities of Brazil,' and Paulo Prado began his interpretation

Retrato de Brasil with the declaration: 'In a radiant land lives a sad people.'[2]

Student: What does the most important sentence tell?

Teacher: It tells us that Brazilians take a close look at themselves. Does it describe how?

Student: It gives two examples. One is a list of 27 unfavorable characteristics and the other is an author's direct quote. What is the author's direct quote?

Teacher: 'In a radiant land lives a sad people.' Which sentence could stand alone?

Student: The first sentence about Brazilians analyzing their own national characteristics. Etc.

In questioning at the paragraph level, our concern is to show relationships between sentences; which sentences can stand alone; which sentences would hardly be missed; and what common thought ties all of the sentences together. The relationship between sentences is more ubiquitous than the idea of searching for the topic sentence. In pure journalistic style, with topic sentences appearing in the first or second line, the topic sentence serves a functional purpose. Not all paragraphs are written in this manner, but all paragraphs do have sentences related in context. Reciprocal questioning explores the strength or weakness of these content relationships.

When dealing with paragraphs, R/Q is likely to result in a greater spread in levels of comprehension. In questioning a very perceptive, mature student there is less need for literal-level questions. With an immature student, many literal- and technical-level questions are necessary. It may be desirable to have an immature student read the whole paragraph aloud before the questioning period to insure that he is capable of doing so.

Reciprocal questioning is not new. Ancient Greeks, Socrates in particular, developed this technique to a fine art in tutorial sessions. Socrates' ultimate aim was to help the student clarify his own thinking and distinguish opinion from knowledge. In contrast, a

---

[2] Lewis Hanke, *South America* (Princeton, N. J.: Van Nostrand Reinhold, 1959), p. 77.

modern R/Q session elicits opinion. The student must make a mental commitment in order to formulate questions. The questioning technique developed by Socrates is still highly regarded today and is referred to as the Socratic or maieutic method.

Another way of analyzing paragraphs is considering them as an aggregate of sentences—mainly descriptive or delineative. To classify paragraphs as one or the other, it is necessary to decide whether the feeling you get is one of being present on the scene (as in a descriptive paragraph) or whether you feel competent to duplicate the scene (as in a delineative paragraph).

DESCRIPTIVE PARAGRAPHS

Descriptive paragraphs help you visualize the scene through use of color, size, temperature, wind, speed, touch, moisture, movement, and sound. Description can be enriched by comparison, contrast, or analogy. Descriptive paragraphs are more typically found in story content. Here is an example of two descriptive paragraphs:

> In appearance, newborn frogs are not what you expect them to be. Instead of looking like tiny frogs, they resemble tiny black fish and are called tadpoles.
>
> Their form changes as they grow in murky, smelly, stagnant waters. They eat seaweed and floating tidbits until one day their back legs begin to grow, then forearms develop and the gills and tail disappear. At this point, they must swim to the surface to breathe. The tadpole is no longer a tadpole; he has turned into a little, green, hopping frog.

DELINEATIVE PARAGRAPHS

In contrast to the above descriptive paragraph, a delineative paragraph contains more organization signals and more specifics. Dimensions such as length, width, and volume are likely to be included. Structure-signaling words such as primary and secondary may appear. Developmental steps and time sequences are listed in an easy-to-follow manner. Sentences defining terms, with several synonyms, are characteristic of this type of paragraph. Recipes, scientific formulas, mathematical problems, and do-it-yourself kits frequently contain delineative paragraphs.

Using essentially the same data as we did in the example of the descriptive paragraph, in the following excerpt structure, organization-signaling words, and measurement have been added. The paragraph could now be more accurately classified as delineative.

> The life cycle of a frog is unusual and includes an egg stage, a gill-breathing stage, and finally a lung-breathing stage. The abundance of eggs is nature's way of combating the hazards of survival. First, the mother frog lays thousands of eggs because chances of the eggs surviving to hatch are not very great. Most of the eggs are eaten by fish or insects. Secondly, the remaining eggs hatch into tadpoles. These tadpoles are less than an inch long and about three-fourths of this is head and body; the remainder is tail. As the tadpole grows, the tail becomes longer in order to propel it in the water. All this time, the swimming tadpole breathes with gills like a fish and looks very much like a tiny fish as he swims around. At about this time, his back legs begin to sprout from his body. Next his forelegs begin to grow and his gills and tail disappear. In this third stage, the tadpole uses his legs to swim to the surface to fill his lungs with air. He is now a fully formed, 1-inch, green frog.

Classification is not always a clear-cut decision. Frequently, paragraphs are such an amalgamation that they are difficult to identify. Analyzing a paragraph carefully is, however, more important than the final classification.

POINT OF VIEW

Another dimension of the paragraph is the point of view from which it is written. Mature elementary students, as well as secondary students, are ready for such diagnosis. They can understand that although the author tells the story through the eyes of a character in the story, he tells you what goes on in the character's mind and how the character feels, and when this happens the author is omniscient. When the author has a plot or article which he wishes to bring close to the reader, he writes in the first person singular. Authors of textbooks may write in the editorial "we." Stories are usually written as seen through the eyes of the leading character or in the third person singular. Interestingly enough, no matter whether the author uses I, we, he, or they, the writer is addressing himself to you, the reader. In fact, no matter how expert the author is in his own field, he must learn how to initiate a two-way conversation. The author asks, "Will the reader understand what I mean or should I tell him more about it?" As the reader reacts to the paragraph he may say, "I'm not sure what happened here, I wish the author had been more specific." As soon as the reader says, "I wonder what this article is about," the page of print can then, and only then, answer his question. The page has nothing to say to the reader until he has enough curiosity to ask something. R/Q is one way of generating this curiosity, and it is also a measure of his involvement. R/Q has been discussed at the sentence and paragraph level, but it is an equally effective device at the story level.

Reciprocal questioning provides a purpose for investigating the ideas and happenings in print at the chapter level, technical article level, or at the literary book level.

Questions will be categorized as follows: those concerning characters and plot are likely to be at the literal level; those relating to causes of feelings and the author's theme are more likely to be interpretative; questions on style tend to be technical ones. An application of the R/Q technique to trade books follows:

After reading the 1961 Newbery-Award-winning book, *Island of the Blue Dolphins,*[3] the following R/Q could take place:

(Literal)	*Student:*	Who wrote the *Island of the Blue Dolphins*?
	Teacher:	Scott O'Dell. Can you tell me who is the main character in the story?
	Student:	Karana. Where does the story take place?
	Teacher:	On the Island of the Blue Dolphins. In three sentences or less can you tell the plot of the story?
	Student:	Karana is accidentally left on the island. After the death of Ramo, her brother, she lives alone in great hardship. After 18 years, she is brought to California by a missionary.
(Interpretative)		What is the theme of this story?
	Teacher:	The author's reverence for life is the theme of the book.
(Interpretative)		Can you think of an example of this?
	Student:	When Karana has a chance to kill Rontu, she cannot.

[3]Scott O'Dell, *Island of the Blue Dolphins* (Boston: Houghton Mifflin, 1960).

(Technical)		How does the author give you the feeling that the Ghalas-ats were a simple people?
	Teacher:	By using simple sentences and by using *said* almost exclusively.
(Interpretative)		Would you have let Rontu live?
	Student:	I think so. I hope so. He was helpful and a comfort to her.
(Interpretative)		Could an Indian girl really live alone like that?
	Teacher:	Possibly, not exactly as the author says, but according to history an Indian girl really did live on an island for 18 years.
(Technical)		Does this book have mainly dialogue or description? Etc.

One of the greatest joys in reading a book is having an opportunity to share what you have read with someone else. Reciprocal questioning gives the student an opportunity to do this.

In a capsule, the reader is the one who brings excitement to the content. By his technical skill and his knowledge of the subject matter, he either enjoys or endures what he is assigned to read. A mathematician may chuckle with delight as he reads through an analysis of variance which a less knowledgeable student would find incomprehensible. On the other hand, this same mathematician might plod through *Dune*,[4] and miss the symbolic references characteristic of this action-packed science fiction.

In retrospect, various techniques are available that lead to the development of a broad base of knowledge. The following activities are effective for this purpose: reciprocal questioning at the sentence, paragraph, and story level; classifying descriptive and delineative paragraphs; and analyzing the author's point of view.

Students who have participated in these techniques will have built a firm foundation upon which to construct future reading habits.

R/Q References

Atkinson, John W. and Norman T. Feather, *A Theory of Achievement Motivation.* New York: John Wiley, 1969.

Guszak, F. J., "Teachers' Questions and Levels of Reading Compre-

[4]Frank Herbert, *Dune* (Philadelphia: Chilton Co., 1965).

hension," in T. C. Barrett, ed., *The Evaluation of Children's Reading Achievement.* Newark, Del.: International Reading Association, 1967.

Manzo, A. V., "The Request Procedure," *Journal of Reading,* Vol. 13, No. 2 (Nov. 1969).

8

WEAVING WORD WITCHERY

Sending students to the dictionary to look up lists of words under the guise of whetting their curiosity is a dead-end assignment. It curbs their curiosity by furnishing them with more information than they care to know and gives them no personal reason for knowing it.

Words cast spells. From the stage, Houdini in his swirling black cape chants "Abracadabra," and a rabbit appears from nowhere. From the pages of fiction, Ali Baba calls "Open sesame," and dazzling treasures surround him.

Off-stage and away from the pages of fiction, *words* are no less powerful. The verdict of "guilty" may deprive a man of his freedom for the rest of his life. The semanticist reminds us that a word is nothing more than a symbol, but it is evident that symbols often have phenomenal impact.

WORD BOUNDARIES

Words have boundaries. The dictionary helps to identify word maps. But when confined to the dictionary, the child pursues a lonely course in search of these boundaries. A more interesting and productive way to learn the mapping of words is by telling about everyday items. A valuable assignment is to ask students to describe as many *tables* as they have ever seen. The variety of responses within a classroom is frequently amazing. Answers include an assortment of *tables* on which to serve food, as well as a wide variety of other kinds of *tables*, such as a multiplication table, a ping-pong table, a pool table, or an operating table. Charting the number of meanings that a single word can have is a good homework assignment. The child should be encouraged to get the information from people he knows. The pupil who has a doctor or nurse in the family may come back with an anatomical meaning of *table* as referring to a part of the bony structure of the skull; the child with an architect or draftsman in his family, may come back with *table* as a protruding horizontal decoration. Some other specialized applications of the word will come from backgammon players (as a backboard), from geologists (as a plateau), from palmists (as the palm of the hand), from jewelers (as the flat surface of a precious stone), and from parliamentarians (as the removal of a bill from consideration). Then, as a final check, children may verify the completeness of their mapping by looking up the word in an inanimate source, the dictionary. Some students may be curious about the origin of the word, and in the *Oxford Dictionary* they can trace the origin through other languages and changes of meaning.

Students can see the analogy between the mapping of a word and the mapping of a river. Like a trickle of water sliding downhill which may deviate according to the terrain, so do words branch off and tumble into various meanings in new word environments.

WHAT'S MY WORD?

Words enter our everyday vocabulary as we use them and understand their meanings. *What's My Word* is a device to stimulate the use and understanding of words. This game employs terms used in everyday activities. The procedure for initiating the game is to choose one child to select a secret word familiar to the class. Each class member is allowed to ask one question which can be answered by a "yes," "no," or "maybe," in order to guess what the word is. The child who guesses correctly becomes the next to select a new word. For example, the following dialogue might take place:

Questions	*Answers*
Do both men and women use it?	Yes
Would I be likely to use this word?	Yes
Is it used three times a day?	Could be
Is it a plate?	No
Is it bigger than a plate?	Yes
Is it a table?	Yes

USEFUL MORPHEMES

Neologism refers to the forming of new words. Through the centuries, words have entered language via many paths. Common sources of change are: (1) adaptations from other languages (love, referring to zero in tennis, comes from the French *l'oeuf*–"egg," zero); (2) changes in meanings of existing words (*rap,* referring to holding intimate conversations or talk sessions); and (3) the coining of new words (*scuba,* referring to self-contained underwater breathing apparatus). In the accelerated tempo of the world of today, these processes are taking place at an ever increasing rate. The preadolescent speeds up the process of language change by making up his own words and giving new meanings to old words. We can capitalize on his impatience with words as they are and help him go beyond his own efforts by encouraging him to combine prefixes, suffixes, and root words to create new words. In doing so, he can familiarize himself with the morphology of his language. By means of this process, he learns hundreds of already existing words, thus broadening his vocabulary.

Morphemes such as the following may be used as tools to build new words:

Prefixes

tele-	distant
ab-	away from, lack of
in (im, il)-	not
pre-	before
anti-	against
re-	again

Roots

logo-	word
loco-	place
phon-	sound
graph-	write
mar-	sea
ology-	study of

Suffixes

ist-	one who
er-	one who
al-	like
ism-	group of
ment-	act of

BREWING NEW WORDS

A suggested assignment is to combine root words with prefixes or suffixes or both, so that the student forms a new word.

Telelogo could refer to words used on a distant planet. A *telelogist* could be one who has a special knowledge of such words.

Abephone could indicate the absence of sound. *Abephonology* would refer to the study of a lack of sound, as in outer space.

The following are examples of possible combinations of morphemes:

Illogo	illogist
Pregraph	pregraphal
Antimar	antimarism

In making up new words, students develop a sophistication in using the dictionary. For example, the dictionary does not list *abph* as a possible spelling. Therefore, in brewing a new word such as *abphone,* it seems more logical to spell the word *abephone* since it is then easier to pronounce. The addition of a vowel creates a third syllable and offers a more euphonious pronunciation, just as *telephone* is easier to pronounce than *telphone.* Student should also be familiar with *e* as a common word ending that often makes the preceding vowel in the syllable long; thus, the English word phone includes an *e* at the end and the newly made-up word would be *abephone* rather than *abephon.*

INTRICACIES OF NEOLOGISMS

The negative form of many words uses the prefix *in.* However, when the root word begins with an *m* or *p,* the student will discover that the *in* is changed to *im* to make the word more pronounceable. Words that begin with *l,* such as *logical,* form their negative by changing the *in* to *il* for easier pronunciation, as in *illogical.* A new word to represent *no place,* would be spelled *illoco* instead of *inloco.* This makes it easier to pronounce and a more plausible English word.

In creating new words, the student should research carefully. Then he should use the new words in his writing.

The following excerpt, written by a student, shows the application of a newly awakened interest in vocabulary:

> News of the approaching visit of a spaceship electrified the earthlings. Messages written in *telelogo* from the planet Leo, were like *illogos* to earthlings. *Telelogists* from language centers had been trying to decode the *telelogos* but without success. Telephotos informed earthlings about the coming visit.
>
> *Hypothetical Glossary*
>
> illogo (il, logo), n. L, il, not, *logo,* word; a nonword such as *nzt.*
>
> telelogo (tel, logo) Gr. tele, far, *logo,* word; words from far away, words from other planets, words at least a hundred light years away.

PRESTIGE WORDS

In addition to the challenge of inventing neologisms, students enjoy bringing in new words they have discovered outside of the classroom. This interest can be put to work by setting aside a mystery-word corner on the blackboard. Establish criteria for its use, such as having the student bring in a word to stump the class which he can pronounce, spell, and use in a sentence. A child might bring in a word such as *pusillanimous.* It is well for the teacher to make sure the child knows the word thoroughly before proceeding. The child then presents it to the class by writing it on the blackboard and also using it in a sentence, thus:

> *Mystery Word:* pusillanimous.
> Girls are sometimes pusillanimous.
>
> In *The Wizard of Oz,* the lion is a pusillanimous beast.

The teacher remains at the front of the room and the child becomes an assistant teacher in the back. As each member of the class tries to guess the pronunciation and its meaning, he may whisper it to either the teacher or the assistant teacher. If he is successful, he in turn becomes an assistant teacher and takes his place in another part of the room. If he is not successful, he returns to his seat and can try again later. In this manner, each child has a chance to become an assistant teacher and help another child. The most difficult task is to teach those children who are able to figure out words easily how to help others who are less adept at working with them. It is well to encourage these student assistants to reinforce the part of the word the child is able to get right, whether it is the beginning, middle, or ending.

SUBSTITUTING WORDS

Another device for developing fluency with words is to work with well-known sayings, such as: "A rolling stone gathers no moss." Ask the students if they can convey the same idea, and at the same time baffle their readers; i.e., *A rotating solid core of mineral matter accumulates a negative amount of small, green bryophytic plants.* Conversely, ask the students to select and copy a long, involved statement from a 19th-century author and see if they can rewrite it as a brief, simple, direct English sentence. Dickens is a good source for selections that lend themselves to this type of activity.

Another suggestion is to copy paragraphs of successful authors with words missing. Ask the students to fill in the blank spaces with appropriate words. After this exercise has been completed, results may be compared with the original selection.

The following is a paragraph taken from *War Beneath the Sea* by Frank Bonham. In this story, Keith Stocker endures the rigors of submarine training in World War II. As a crewman on the *U.S.S. Mako* he is assigned to patrol the dangerous Pacific waters. The paragraph describes the sub immediately after it is hit by an aerial bomb.

> Wrenched by the detonation, the sub went __________. Someone ______________ on the emergency lamps. Another bomb exploded farther forward and ______________ the boat sharply down by the bow. Mako's dive was suddenly a ______________ angle for the bottom.[1]

Check to see how many of the author's words were used: dark, cut, tipped, and headlong. What excitement for the students who select some of the same words the author used. Students will develop a sensitivity for the appropriateness of some words when compared with others. No author is infallible in his use of words, and yet a successful author more often uses appropriate rather than inappropriate words.

WORD WITCHERY

From the cauldron
    of witch's brew
The word is old
    the meaning's new.

Throughout history, each succeeding generation has influenced the language patterns of the times. This is especially true today with the increasing number of new meanings for old words.

A fascinating game to acquaint students with this phenomena follows:

Divide the class into two groups. The teacher presents, from a prepared list, words that have taken on new meanings. Alternate

---

[1] Frank Bonham, *War Beneath the Sea* (New York: Thomas Y. Crowell Co., 1962), p. 104. Used by permission.

students from each side give as many new meanings of the word as they can by using them in a sentence. A sample of common words with new meanings is included here:

Old Word	*New Meaning*
rock	musical beat
cool	right, appealing
happening	spectacular event
brass	top man
swinging	lively
groove	on the right track
rap	to talk with

A similar activity may be built around the use of homographs, such as the following:

présent	presént
áddress	addréss
réfuse	refúse
délegate	delegáte
eńvelope	envélope

The teacher may give the student a homograph and ask him to use it in a sentence. The next student may be asked to express a different meaning in a sentence by giving the word a different intonation.

These devices contribute to an awareness of the power of words. The more that students know about words, the more tools they have to express their own ideas and interpret the writings of others. Students learn that word meanings are controlled by word boundaries, word intonations, and word environments.

WORD SETS

Word sets are groups of words that can be described. They constitute another way of looking at words just as number sets constitute another way of looking at numbers. Words are related by sound systems, structure, and meanings. One of the values derived from working with word sets according to sound and structure is better understanding of the phonemes and morphemes of the English language. Word sets which emphasize meaning help to enrich the student's vocabulary by focusing on dimensions and relationships; such as, analogies, word ratios, antonyms, synonyms, homonyms, and categorizations.

The following is a list of words that students may classify into other word sets:

The above word lists can be divided into additional sets of words, a few of which might be as follows:

1. Emphasizing sound of words (initial consonant)

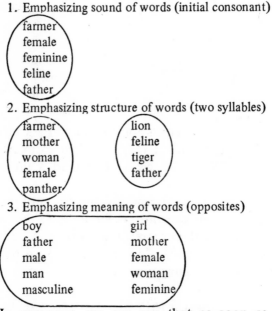

farmer
female
feminine
feline
father

2. Emphasizing structure of words (two syllables)

farmer	lion
mother	feline
woman	tiger
female	father
panther	

3. Emphasizing meaning of words (opposites)

boy	girl
father	mother
male	female
man	woman
masculine	feminine

In summary, we can say that as soon as students realize the fascination and excitement of *wordology,* their interest and knowledge will burst with the potential of more effective communication through expanded reading. Words are catalysts which we employ to control our environment, and they in turn control us.

Wild, wonderful words weave wizardry!

Reference Books

Bodmar, Frederick and Lancelot Hogben, *The Loom of Language,* New York: Norton and Co., Inc., 1944.

Chase, Stuart, *The Tyranny of Words,* New York: Harcourt, Brace & World, 1938.

Funk, Charles, *Thereby Hangs a Tale: Stories of Curious Word Origins,* New York: Harper & Row, 1950.

Garey, Doris, *Putting Words in Their Places,* Glenview, Ill.: Scott, Foresman, 1957.

Girsdansky, Michael, *The Adventure of Language.* New York: Prem. Fawcett World, 1963.

Onions, C. T., ed., *Oxford Dictionary of English Etymology.* New York: Harper & Row, 1950.

PART III

PLACING A VALUE ON READING

REVIVING HOPE

Failure to read is a blight that spreads through all academic learning. The sight of a book causes an emotional response so strong that a child's readiness to read is lost. Such a child needs to be introduced to materials and methods other than those which he has learned to associate with failure.

Hope is vital in learning to read. The child who considers reading a hopeless task is defeated before he has a chance to learn. Since the development of attitude is of utmost importance, we should provide leverage to change negative feelings to positive feelings. All sources affecting the child should work toward the same goal; namely, that of changing a child's defeatist attitude into a hopeful one.

PARENTS PARTICIPATE

In utilizing all available resources, it is well to begin with the home. Remember, parents function best in a supportive rather than a teaching role. There are many misconceptions commonly held by parents. They usually believe that small words are synonymous with easy words. As adults they know these service words so well it is inconceivable to them that such words could be demons for their children. Chances are they do not know what a digraph is, and so they have no way of knowing a single reason why *when* and *then* are confusing to children. Yet, if parents were asked to act out these words, sketch them, locate them on a map, or even define them, they would be at a loss to do so. These two words like most of the 220 words on the Dolch Basic List[1] are difficult for children to master. These two words are difficult to visualize. The differences between them are so minute that they are indistinguishable to the untrained eye. Parents may show impatience as they listen to the child read, and the child will feel defeated.

Parents who cannot be supportive should not attempt to conduct a tutoring session. To compound the difficulty the child frequently makes incorrect associations, such as substituting *where* for *there*. The task of breaking an incorrect association is more difficult than introducing the word slowly enough the first time to allow the child to make a habit of correct association. The whole process can be likened to buying a lot clear and ready to build as opposed to buying one with a poor structure already on it. This makes it necessary to spend time and effort to tear down the inadequate structure on the latter lot before a new building can be started.

Another misconception is that parents often think that if a child can learn prestige words such as *Hawaii* or *alligator,* he can learn the Dolch words more easily, when in fact the reverse is true.

Parents can help by reinforcing learnings. After the child is fairly comfortable with the sounds that have been taught in school, a Parent-Participation Sheet can be sent home. This sheet will inform parents of the sounds that have been presented in school, and will permit them to reinforce these sounds by sketching or cutting out pictures from magazines of objects which begin with these sounds.

Mm *Parent-Child Activity.*
Cut out or draw objects
that begin with m, such
as moon, map, and marbles.

After the child can pronounce and understand the following words and phrases, send Bingo Games home like the following:

Directions: Two copies of each of the following bingo cards should be sent home. One set contains words and the other set contains phrases. Instruct

[1] E. W. Dolch, *Dolch Sight Vocabulary Cards* (Champaign, Ill.: Garrard Press, n.d.).

the parent to cut up one of the word cards and one of the phrase cards. To play word bingo, mix words and call them one at a time. The child covers the words called on the remaining card with a bean or penny. (One possible incentive is to allow him to keep the pennies.) Phrase bingo is played in the same manner.

this	want	we
can	free	go
saw	with	the

this boy	want a toy	we can
can run	free toy	go here
saw you	with her	the car

Few parents have the information or technical skill to introduce learning that a child may find difficult. On the other hand, most parents would, in the spirit of fun and partnership, be able to reinforce learnings that were already a part of the child's knowledge. By reinforcing the correct responses, the child will gain in speed, accuracy, and self-confidence. A child's comprehension is dependent partly on rapid recognition of words. Unless high-frequency words are learned at the automatic response level, the child will be at a loss to comprehend what he reads since he will be too hampered by decoding.

Parents can help, in general, by being supportive and not impatient, making books available to the child, and setting an example as an adult who enjoys reading. They can specifically help by being volunteer parents in the classroom. As they understand the purpose of developing independent readers, they can help in checking out paired partners as described later in this chapter.

READING CENTER

Parents can help by contributing comfortable furniture to a reading center. Colorful cushions, an area rug, and chairs soft and big enough to curl up in can do much toward making a section of an ordinary classroom into an attractive and inviting retreat. Bookcases of various heights are usually available in most schools, and if not, these can be constructed at very little cost. The freedom to choose from a wide selection of books, and possibly to stretch full length on a rug—with elbows propped on a pillow—goes a long way toward making reading a pleasant experience. The use of such a haven may be regarded as a privilege by students.

BULLETIN BOARDS

Student bulletin boards are another valuable part of the environment because they can be an integral part of learning. They constitute an opportunity for enriching all phases of the reading program. When coordinated with instruction, they can fit into an active learning plan in a number of ways. A bulletin board with the caption CAN YOU TOP THIS?—filled with words to be placed in sentences—is one such productive working-board idea. A sprinkling of nouns, verbs, adverbs, and adjectives (a few of which are prestige words) can be shuffled and recombined into numerous sentences. A "special privilege" is given to the student who can top all others by submitting the longest list of completed sentences. This award can take the form of receiving a coveted honor, such as serving as chairman of a class meeting or acting as a team leader at recess time.

Topics for student bulletin boards, then, may reflect almost any learning activity, such as: prestige words, illustrated sentences, talking walls (conversations overheard and written on sentence strips—to be matched later with the correct person), directions for performing tasks, and the typical work-display material. Students respond and are encouraged to sketch plans and actually put up their creative efforts, as a small group activity. This usually means that students and teachers plan together so that there is a tie-in between subject matter and display.

CLASSROOM PARTICIPATION

A supportive classroom climate can provide an *esprit de corps* so that the entire class gets excited by the success of even the slowest of its members. The total emphasis changes from inner competitiveness to cooperation. The strength of this program is based upon multiplying the number of forces that facilitate learning. In a classroom of 31 children, instead of one full-time teacher you have the teacher plus 30 assistants. Under a well-planned program, every child at some time experiences the role of teacher. Children are more apt to react positively to reading in such a rich learning environment than if the teacher is the authority figure and the only dispenser of knowledge.

PAIRED PARTNERS

One type of supportive program is paired partners. This method, which compounds the number of teachers in the classroom, needs to be initiated slowly. Begin by selecting the best reader in the classroom.

1. Tell the child he can choose whatever story he wants to read aloud.
2. Have him choose a classmate who would enjoy reading the story with him.
3. Go to a part of the room that is as far from the rest of the class as possible.

Teacher supervises following procedure:

a. One child reads the title and author.
b. Both children look at the illustrations on the first few pages.
c. From the title and the pictures, they try to figure out what the story plot is and how the story will end.
d. Next, they take turns reading a page of the story.
e. After completing the story, they compare their prediction with the actual ending.
f. If the child who is reading aloud does not know a word, he may:
   (1) skip the word and read the rest of the sentence;
   (2) wait for his partner to give him a clue, such as, "it begins like ________, or it rhymes with ________, or it means ________;"
   (3) listen as his partner tells him the word.

By selecting an outstanding reader as a member of the first paired partners, the activity gains prestige. Let the first pair demonstrate for the class. As other children ask for the privilege or seem capable of working in pairs, choose additional couples to work in this way. In a class of 30, this means that as many as 15 children could be reading aloud simultaneously from different stories. The room will have a high but constructive noise level.

There are several advantages to coupling students as paired partners. For one thing, members of the class have seen the best readers in the room demonstrate how much fun such an activity can be. Another factor is that each pair has the privilege of reading a story of his own choice. Students work with a friend of their own choosing. Interestingly enough, children tend to choose partners of about the same reader level. The act of reading together is more helpful than reading alone because each child has an audience as well as someone with whom to share the humor or excitement of the story. Also, there are two persons instead of one to figure out difficult words.

To become fluent, children need opportunities to read aloud. In a typical 20-minute reading group of ten children, each child is limited to 2 minutes of oral reading; whereas, in paired partners *every* child in the room has the opportunity to read aloud, possibly five times as long. And finally, a child is not likely to retain a negative attitude toward reading in such a free-choice activity.

DE-EMPHASIZE ABILITY GROUPING

Since negative readers often are found in the low-ability group in reading, it is essential to discuss grouping practices. Children should rarely, if ever, be grouped in a low-ability group because that will make them feel defeated. For this reason, it is important to explore grouping practices other than ability grouping. The three standard, inflexible ability groups common throughout the country are deadly for all, but particularly for the low group. Average or above-average children can gain from *some* ability grouping since they already have self-confidence. All students can gain from grouping that is kept flexible by the teacher, or by multi-based grouping, as described later. Flexible grouping is economical of the teacher's time and should definitely have a place in the classroom schedule, regardless of the teacher's instructional approach to reading.

The fact that children are aware of differences in reading ability in the classroom is not in itself harmful, but constant reminders by the teacher can place an unrealistic emphasis on the individual's ranking.

The teacher who makes remarks such as, "If you miss any more school, I will drop you back to John's group," is inadvertently exaggerating the differences in ability. Seemingly innocuous remarks like this could create an insurmountable barrier and might cause the child to withdraw from the learning situation completely.

We function in a world of mixed ability groups. Education has no right to be stratified in an artificial manner. The less capable readers, in the hands of skillful teachers, are frequently stimulated to performance beyond that which they would normally attain if confined in a homogeneous group. The trend today is to incorporate even physically handicapped children into regular classrooms. It is of paramount importance that we do not segregate and label our crippled readers.

At the turn of this century, Betts[2] made a strong plea for flexible and multi-based groupings. Today our schools still represent a 20-year lag. Teachers who profess to have flexible ability grouping, but who have three groups and shift no more than three to five children during the course of a year, have, in fact, inflexible groups.

Slow-paced readers should be treated mainly as individuals or as paired readers. These individuals may be grouped for work on special projects, such as reading a mail-order catalogue to discover the best bicycle to buy or preparing a story to read aloud to members of a grade below them. They can be invited to join other ability groups and, instead of preparing a play or a story, they would be asked to prepare a paragraph or a sentence, or even a phrase in accordance with their ability. At other times in the day, they can be paired or incorporated into a boy or girl group which is learning word-attach skills through playing phonics games. While participating in ability, interest, and skill-development groups, expectations of what they will contribute *must* be realistic. Always and forever, the teacher should give these slow-paced students a chance to share what they know, and she should introduce new words at a rate and by a method commensurate with their ability and style of learning.

Total group reading must be conducted as a multi-level session. It is particularly valuable to use the entire class in the introduction of a new topic or in review work. There are many other types of learning which benefit from such presentations, such as choral verse, class newspaper, *Weekly Reader*, and current events.

Suggested multi-based grouping patterns that minimize ability grouping are as follows:

Multi-Based Groupings

Makeup of the Groups	*Possible Content*
Boys	Do-it-yourself models (such as a ready-to-assemble birdhouse) Adventure stories Mysteries Tall tales

[2]Emmett Betts, *Foundations of Reading Instruction* (New York: American Book Company, 1946), pp. 390-394.

Girls	Easy recipes Romantic stories
Artistic children	Appropriate reading level Caldecott-Award-winning books
Literary children	Appropriate reader level in the Newbery-Award-winning books (this activity is more appropriate for grades 5 and 6)
Children with a good sense of humor	Joke books Riddle books Humorous stories
Children lacking specific skills	Drills that stress suffixes and other problem areas

Master teachers strive to avoid a negative reaction and aim to strengthen the child's hope of success in reading. In the primary grades, these teachers plan several reading opportunities and arrange for individuals or paired partners to read aloud at least once a day. The teacher meets with each child as a member of some type of group. Friday is usually a multi-level, total-class, new reading period. Instructional-level reading groups function best with approximately six children, and for that reason we recommend four groups at the primary level.

Independent reading groups are different from paired partners, in that the child who is selected as the teacher is a reader level above the other children in the group. However, the procedure for figuring out a new word is the same as that used with paired partners. The child in the role of teacher follows the same steps for figuring out new words as in paired partners. She also:

1. Helps the children find the right page.
2. Asks them to tell what they think the story is about.
3. Gives credit to outstanding features of the oral reader, such as:
   "You sounded just like the angry troll."
   "You didn't miss a single word."
   "When you read about the cave, you made it sound dark and scary."

By following this sample plan (facing page), it is evident that most of the primary child's school day is spent in learning to read. This is his most critical academic task. His most important affective learning is to develop a feeling of self-worth. One way to increase his

Sample Reading Plan for Primary Grades

Mon.	*Tues.*	*Wed.*	*Thurs.*	*Fri.*
1. Top and Average Instructional Groups 2. Individuals	1. Top and Average Instructional Groups 2. Individuals	1. Top and Average Instructional Groups 2. Individuals	Oriental Blab-School (Reading all at Same Time)	News Total Class
Independent Groups	Independent Groups	Independent Groups	or Paired Partners	Individual Silent Reading or Paired or Applied Reading*
Paired Partners Oral Reading	Paired Partners Oral Reading	Paired Partners Oral Reading		

*Applied reading means that the reading leads to an activity such as building a model, making a pudding, or acting out a play.

self-esteem is to share information with others. The paired partner who formulates clues to help another child experiences a sense of accomplishment. The partner who receives the clues must apply them and thus he also retains a feeling of self-importance.

So far in this chapter, we have stressed the value of a positive approach in developing a child's hopeful attitude by enlisting the cooperation of parents, emulating methods of master primary teachers, and providing varied reading opportunities.

While it is not probable, it is possible that in spite of supportive parents and master teachers, a child may decide it is more profitable to "not read" than to read. It is at this point that the teacher has a child with an attitude problem on her hands. In the case of a child who is passive-aggressive, he may be outwardly complacent and agreeable while inwardly rejecting reading.

In working with a child of this type, whatever the cause of his resistance to reading might be, his attitude must be changed. If inwardly he has decided reading is not for him, he becomes an academic dropout. One way to reach such a child is through non-school-oriented reading tasks, such as feeling, manipulating, decoding, and profit-centered activities. In fact, game-oriented activities are especially appropriate. It is hoped that these non-academic activities will be effective in replacing negative influences with positive responses. As the child succeeds in learning through essentially nonacademic techniques, he soon becomes a changed person with renewed hope as a result of new basic skills.

In some instances, the child loses hope because he has unrealistic aspirations. The child who is unfairly compared with an older sibling may need to be helped to set realistic goals for himself. If after one year of school he only learned to read his name, he is likely to need letter- and word-matching activities. Set up a criterion performance graph based on five correctly matched letters out of five tries. Keep a record of the letters on the vertical axis, and the number of days spent learning them on the horizontal axis. (See graph at bottom of facing page.)

In the accompanying graph, the child took three days to pass the criterion performance for the letter B and five days to learn C and F. Each child's progress report should be appropriate to his individual needs.

Records of achievement may be kept at different levels. Suggested achievement goals follow:

Perception of form	Phrase reading
Perception of sound	Sentence reading
Letter matching	Paragraph reading
Letter naming	Comprehension:
Word matching	1. Factual
Word reading	2. Interpreted
	3. Applied
	4. Extended

Ordinarily, the teacher inadvertently penalizes the child who reads poorly in two ways: by presenting work assignments in written form, and by rewarding completion of the initial assignment with additional tasks to be read and completed. Work and more work is hardly conducive to reading more effectively. Occasionally written directions should contain a bonus, such as: "After you finish your assignment, you may paint a picture or listen to the records." Some children are better reached through the stomach, so they may select a graham cracker or a cookie. Active children may choose to play a game such as ring toss. But whatever surprise or bonus is offered, it should be written out for them to read.

To summarize, bonus assignments are best presented in written

PROGRESS REPORT IN LETTER MATCHING

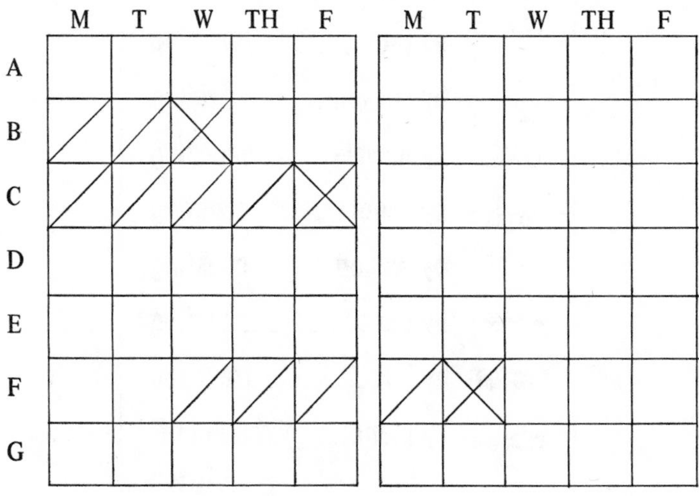

form, but regular work assignments should be given orally, at least for slow readers.

Another technique used by master teachers is switching roles with the child. The child learns the skill at a deeper level of understanding. If the skill taught was the medial *a* as in m*a*t, c*a*t, or r*a*t, the child in the role of the teacher would have to think of new words to test the "make believe" student—words such as *fa*t, *pa*t, and *sa*t. It is difficult to think of new words fitting this same pattern or ways to use words already known. Therefore, when the child does this successfully, he gains understanding and feelings of self-esteem.

Even a slow learner may benefit by helping a child less able than himself. If a slow starter goes to the kindergarten to teach a younger child how to tie a bow, trace a letter, or copy his name, the activity gives the slow student status. Even though the tasks he teaches do not directly involve reading, it is likely that his own feeling of self-confidence will be reflected in increased reading ability.

Another valuable device of master teachers is the use of reading charts. They incorporate vocabulary and concepts which will be needed by children in their writing and reading. The following is an illustration of a Social Studies multi-level vocabulary chart:

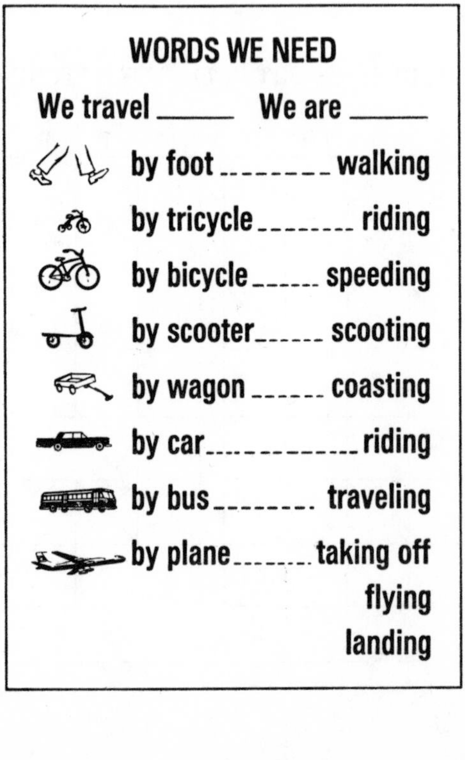

WORDS WE NEED

We travel ____	We are ____
by foot	walking
by tricycle	riding
by bicycle	speeding
by scooter	scooting
by wagon	coasting
by car	riding
by bus	traveling
by plane	taking off
	flying
	landing

As opposed to this well-planned technique, the teacher who does not organize and writes words only as children request them has a board filled with a hodge-podge. The children have difficulty in locating the words on the board and consequently exasperate the teacher by asking for the same words over again. The preceding reference chart classifies words so that nouns and verbs are grouped together. The similar patterns in *tricycle* and *bicycle* and in verbs ending in "ing" are made easy to identify by being placed close enough for visual comparison. Reading is built upon concepts, and unless a child has a frame of reference leading from the known to the

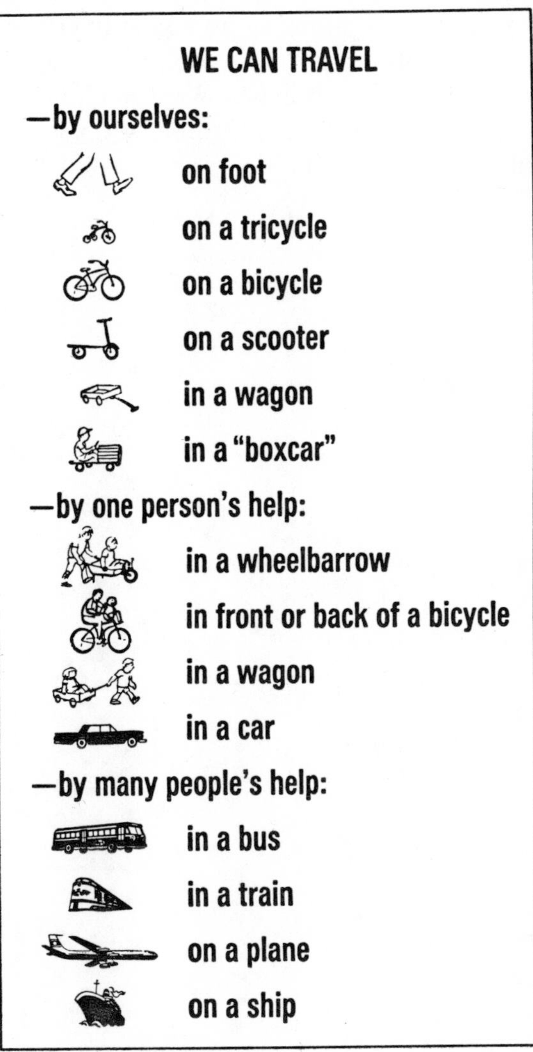
WE CAN TRAVEL
—by ourselves:
on foot
on a tricycle
on a bicycle
on a scooter
in a wagon
in a "boxcar"
—by one person's help:
in a wheelbarrow
in front or back of a bicycle
in a wagon
in a car
—by many people's help:
in a bus
in a train
on a plane
on a ship

unknown, he is incapable of understanding concepts. A means of conveying this to the child is to set up an organizational chart which leads from what the child knows best to what he knows least. The illustration on page 147 could be used in a Social Studies unit.

As the child reads books about travel his fluency and comprehension are increased, since he knows the vocabulary and can categorize travel in different ways.

If we would emulate the techniques of the master teacher, we would never lose hope for a single child in the class, we would build strength where there is weakness. Through resource charts we would preplan to insure successful reading experiences for the child. Above all, we would be flexible and have no commitment to a single-tract system but use whatever is appropriate from all the materials, methods, and techniques available. We would make use of non-academic procedures as well as unorthodox classroom practices in order to build hope, self-confidence, and ultimately, success in reading.

10

READING AND RELUCTANT READERS

Reluctant readers, by their actions, are screaming their abhorrence of reading. Although they may tell an adult, "I love to read," their actions expose them. If they read at all, these children read in strained voices, a halting manner, and in obvious discomfort. They do not love anything about reading.

By reluctant readers we mean children who are physically and mentally capable of reading, who *can* read but who avoid books and read only under duress. Basically they are responding to aspirations that are unrealistic, and this causes them to be dissatisfied with their own performance.

Some of the many ruses of reluctant readers are compulsive talking, excuse making, rationalizing, and blaming. Other signs of the reluctant reader may include psychosomatic illness, silliness, aggressiveness, and shyness.

The children cited in the following four cases are products of four different reading approaches. In each case, the particular method was found to be inappropriate for the child. These cases are taken from the files of the San Diego State College Clinical Training Center and represent two semesters of remediation, or approximately 40 sessions. Each child was assigned an individual student teacher to serve as a clinician working under the direct supervision of the Training Center staff. Each file contains an initial interview with one of the parents of the child, plus other data which demonstrate that reluctant readers *can* become interested readers.

RELUCTANT READER REPORTS

Clinic Attendance

A full semester consists of 22 after-school sessions of 50 minutes each.

I. Classroom-Reading Approach: Individualized Reading

Student: Brian J.	Age: 10	WISC Verbal	104
Grade	5	Performance	108
Actual Grade	5.5	Full Scale	107
WRAT (Reading)	2.8	Vineland Social Quotient (S.Q.)	109
Difference	−2.7		

Formula of Average Gain per Year

Average Gain per Year = AG
Actual Grade = Ac
WRAT Reading Score = WRS

$$Ac \overline{)\,WRS}^{\;AG} \qquad 5.5 \overline{)\,2.8}^{\;.51}$$

To date, Brian gained in his ability to decode words an average of five months for each year he attended school.

Problem: Inability to decode words in isolation.

Comprehension: Brian uses context clues, so he does better when he reads in context than when he tries to decode words in isolation. His score on Gray's Oral Reading Paragraphs is 3.2.

Mother's Report: "The teachers have been telling us not to worry, that Brian is no problem in school except that he likes to talk to his neighbors, but we know he has a reading problem. I know that it is *not* typical for a boy to avoid reading so completely. Brian never reads at home. When I visited school and his class was supposed to be reading library books, he was merely flipping the pages."

Initial Interview: Brian is a good looking, blond boy; he is taller and heavier than most fifth-grade boys. He loves playing baseball and going camping with the family. Brian enjoys being at home and gets along well with the children in the neighborhood and at school. He loves to joke and has a good sense of humor. His mother works, so he's quite independent, and this is reflected in his high social quotient. He has never done well in any school subject since all are more or less dependent upon reading. He has begun complaining of stomachaches and headaches to keep from attending school. Later in the day, he is fine.

Initial Clinical Session: The goal was to provide Brian with an accepting attitude so that he would talk freely. It turned out that Brian needed no encouragement. He is a compulsive talker. The suggestion that he read a sentence from a book launched him into a lengthy account of a narrow escape he and his uncle had the previous summer. This boy has an endless flow of thought that rambles on with barely a pause for breath. *In the clinician's words*: "As a listener, I felt exhilarated and frustrated–exhilarated because, in spite of persistent failure, Brian's manner of dealing with his problem was not entirely negative, but was expressed in spontaneous accounts of his experiences; frustrated because his constant flow of words prevented me from guiding the interview."

San Diego Quick Assessment–Brian J.

Grade Level	*Substitution*	*Stimulus Word*	*Errors–Analysis*
1	street	road	(similar meaning–no decoding clues)
2	quick	quietly	(similar configuration and beginning–incorrect ending)
3	town	city	(similar meaning–no decoding)
3	shouted	exclaimed	(similar meaning–wrong beginning and medial sounds)
3	right	straight	(similar ending–wrong beginning)

Test Placement: On words in isolation, Brian can read at high second-grade level. His WRAT score of 2.8 corroborates this finding.

Error Analysis: Of the five errors, three have a similar meaning but are completely different in configuration and sound-letter relationship. The two remaining errors are words with similar configurations: quick - quiet; right - straight. Four out of five errors have incorrect initial sounds. We can thus say that Brian needs help with:

1. Beginning sounds.
2. The *ly* endings.
3. Medial and end sounds.

Hypotheses to Be Tested:

1. Brian memorizes easily. The words he knows he has memorized without using any sound-letter clues.

2. He tends to be overly dependent upon content clues, and relies *too much* on memory and too little on sound-letter relationships.
3. He will change his negative feeling about reading if he associates pleasant experiences with reading.

Final Report of Spring Session: At the end of the semester, the San Diego Quick Assessment was readministered. Brian still scored second grade but he did not make any errors in grade-one material. However, he made an error in grade two (similar to the one made in the pretest) of *quickly* for *quietly*, and he read the word *city* which he missed before. So, while his grade level was the same, his errors were no longer the result of his dependence upon meaning. They were closer to the letter-sound relationship. The clinician reported no substitution of initial consonants by the end of the first semester. The most rewarding change was the fact that Brian no longer felt it necessary to talk his way out of every reading situation in which he found himself. His mother reported that he read the comics at home and that he even bought comic books with part of his allowance. We thus could say that the biggest change in Brian was in his attitude.

Final Report of Fall Session: During this session, the clinician reviewed initial-word sounds and taught word endings of *s, ed, ing,* and *ly*. One of the most successful lessons during this semester began with the reading by the clinician of a six-page account of Babe Ruth's life. Brian dictated what he understood of the story for the clinician to type. The boy was so proud of his one-page account of Babe Ruth's life, and he read it so many times during the semester, that the page was worn thin.

Brian's San Diego Quick Assessment at the end of this semester was at the fourth-reader level. Therefore, while the first semester resulted primarily in an attitude change, the last semester produced positive academic improvement. The WRAT score at the end of the second semester was 4.8, which represents a two-year gain over a one-year period. This score can be appreciated if we compare it with his .5 growth per year before entering the clinic.

II. Classroom-Reading Approach: Basal Reader

Student: John S.	Age: 6	WISC	Verbal 124
Grade	2		Performance 120
Actual Grade	2.2		Full Scale 124
WRAT (Reading)	kg. .9		

Formula of Average Gain per Year

Average Gain per Year = AG
Actual Grade = Ac
WRAT Reading Score = WRS

$$\begin{array}{r} AG \\ Ac\overline{)\,WRS} \end{array} \qquad \begin{array}{r} .41 \\ 2.2\overline{)\,kg.\ .9} \end{array}$$

After one year of academic instruction, John made a .4 gain.

Problem: Visual perception.

Gilmore Oral Comprehension: 1.5.

Mother's Report: "John did not learn to read with the mundane stories in the basal readers. He didn't think they were interesting. He enjoys looking at the cartoons in the New Yorker. We know he is a bright and intelligent boy and it worries us that he hasn't learned to read. We offered to buy him a bicycle when he was in kindergarten if he would just learn his A-B-C's, but he couldn't learn them. All of our children are bright, but they had trouble in learning to read. My husband and I are both college graduates and this failure to read disturbs us."

Initial Interview: John is blond and good looking. He has regular features with a few freckles, and he is taller than the other boys in his class. He likes to draw interesting abstracts which he downgrades. He is the fastest runner in his class.

John said, "I can't read. I'm dumb." It was not easy to get him to talk. He answered with one word whenever possible.

Initial Clinical Session: The clinician was warm and accepting with John, who remained taciturn during most of the period. Since John's answers were all monosyllabic, the clinician had a difficult time establishing rapport. Toward the end of the period, the clinician asked John whether anyone in his family ever read to him. At this time, John said that his father read to him about the gooney birds on Wake Island. His one area of interest seemed to be science, and he explored the canyon behind his home whenever he was allowed to do so. He said he hated reading, and it was obvious that he did. The reward of a bicycle for learning the alphabet (26 nonsense symbols) was seen as a hopeless goal when John was in kindergarten, as indeed it was.

San Diego Quick Assessment–John S.

Grade Level

RR[1]	RR[2]
missed SQ WM	missed all but *j*

Test Placement: John is placed at reading-readiness level 1, which means he still needs practice in finding letters that are alike. He is barely ready for reading-readiness level 2. The only letter he can name is the first letter of John, his name.

Hypotheses:

1. John lives up to the family's expectation that he will not be a reader.
2. John has visual perception problems–he tends to reverse letters and numbers.
3. He has a muscular eye imbalance that adds to his visual problems.

Recommended Procedure:

1. The procedure recommended for John is to effect a change in his role expectation. By using the Peabody Rebus Reading Program[1] or a system made up by the clinician and John, he should be able to combine his name with action pictures. Have John read picto-strips that will baffle his classmates.
2. Have John make an alphabet book composed of pictures of animals plus the first letter in each name.
3. Encourage John to look for letters found in his name on cereal boxes, on billboards, and in the newspaper.
4. Build an index file with letters or rebus words as John learns them.
5. Play games of any kind in which John groups pictures of things that begin in the same way.

---

[1] Richard W. Woodcock, *et al, The Peabody Rebus Reading Program* (Circle Pines, Minn.: American Guidance Services, Inc., 1968).

6. As soon as John learns a word, let him see how many times he can find and circle it in the newspaper.

Final Report of Spring Session: At the end of the semester, the San Diego Quick Assessment was readministered. John scored at reading-readiness level 3, and he correctly identified the five following words on the preprimer list: *play, run, and, look, can.*

John's sight vocabulary had been built up to 16 words. He knew all the letters of the reading readiness list except *h* and *w*. His attitude was changed from one of avoiding all reading situations by saying, "I can't," to one of hopefulness and willingness to try all words that the clinician presented.

John's mother reported that he pointed out the letters from the billboards as they drove by, and that he was interested in the letters on the cereal boxes at the breakfast table.

Final Report of Fall Session: At this time, John was beginning to feel comfortable with words that began with the same letter as his name and the following five initial consonant sounds: j, h, n, s, and hard c.

The most successful games used with John were: Fish, Concentration, and Initial-Consonant Bingo.

John is just beginning to recognize words comfortably in context. When John writes, it is still necessary to have him trace the letters in order to prevent him from reversing them. John is considerably more interested in letters and words than he was before attending the clinic. He can now recognize words that begin with j, h n, s, and hard c.

III. Classroom-Reading Approach: Language Experience

Student: Peter L.	Age: 8	WISC Verbal	94
Grade	3	Performance	104
Actual Grade	3.6	Full Scale	99
WRAT (Reading)	1.2	Vineland Social Quotient (SQ)	103
Difference	−2.4		

Formula of Average Gain per Year

Average Gain per Year = AG
Actual Grade = Ac
WRAT Reading Score = WRS

$$\begin{array}{r} AG \\ Ac \overline{)\,WRS} \end{array} \qquad \begin{array}{r} .33 \\ 3.6 \overline{)\,1.20} \end{array}$$

Average gain per year is .33 months.

Problem: Needs more structure than his classroom teacher provides.

Comprehension: Peter has no word-attack skills and many word confusions—words incorrectly associated; consequently, he cannot read a single paragraph on the Gilmore Oral Reading Test.

Mother's Report: "He has books from the drugstore but Peter don't want to read nothing. He brings home writing papers but he don't even read them. His grandmother bought him *Tom Sawyer*, and he don't even sit still to listen to the story. The teacher tries to explain this writing and writing all day long, but I can't see how it'll ever help Peter learn to read. All the other kids in my family learned to read easy out of those reading books like we had. But this writing business makes Peter sick. I'm getting sick of it too."

Initial Interview: Peter has large, brown eyes, dark skin, and jet-black hair. He is scrubbed so clean he shines. He is one of the shortest boys in the class. He is well liked in the classroom, but in playground activities he is often involved in fighting.

Peter is better than average in computation, but fails miserably when the computation occurs in a reading problem. Every morning for the past week he has been nauseated before going to school.

Initial Clinical Session: The clinician asked Peter to write his name on a piece of paper. Peter said, "If this is going to be another one of those writing schools, I don't want to come here." The clinician assured Peter that it was not.

Peter knows the name of six of the 26 letters: a, b, c, p, t, r. The clinician gave Peter a Bender-Gestalt Visual-Motor Perception Test and the boy enjoyed copying the nine figures successfully. The clinician suggested that during the rest of the semester they would be playing games and matching pictures and, as soon as Peter was ready, they would be reading from books. Peter departed anticipating the next meeting.

San Diego Quick Assessment—Peter L.

Grade Level	*Substitution*	*Stimulus*	*Errors*
PP	there	here	the initial *h* is not identified
Primer	like	work	initial *wor* is not identified as in *word*
	his	this	the initial digraph *th* is not identified
1st	take	thank	initial digraph *th* and phonogram *ank*

Grade Level	*Substitution*	*Stimulus*	*Errors*
	aways	always	initial *al* as in *almost* is missed
	thing	spring	consonant blend *spr* is not identified

Test Placement: Primer level.

Error Analysis: Of the six substitutions, all have initial-sound-syllable errors. All of the errors have correct consonant-sound endings; even the substitution of *take* for *thank*, while spelled differently, has the same end-consonant sound. Peter needs help with:

1. Beginning sounds, such as *h* and *w*.
2. Beginning syllables, such as *al* as in *al*most and *al*though.
3. The consonant blend *spr*.
4. The digraph *th*, as in *th*ink.
5. The phonogram *ank*, as in *bank, tank,* and *rank.*

Hypotheses to Be Tested:

1. Peter is too dependent on the clues provided by end sounds.
2. Peter is confused by a language-experience approach to reading since he lacks the knowledge of initial sounds.
3. Peter is becoming so overwhelmed by the amount of unstructured reading in a language-experience approach that he is developing psychosomatic symptoms.

Recommended Procedure: The recommended procedure for Peter is to provide security through structure. A few suggestions follow:

1. Teach the initial-consonant sounds, and at the same time stress meaning.
2. Teach medial sounds and at the same time stress meaning.
3. Assess progress frequently.
4. Teach words from a preprimer-level trade book before allowing the child to read from the trade book.
5. Inform the parents of the type of books that Peter should be reading and advise them of the inappropriateness of difficult books like *Tom Sawyer*.
6. Encourage Peter to keep a card file of the words he masters.
7. Encourage Peter to look for words that he knows on billboards, TV, and cereal boxes.
8. Give Peter the opportunity to read an easy preprimer trade book to younger children.

Final Report of Spring Semester: The post-test score on the San Diego Quick Assessment placed Peter at the second-grade reader level. This reflected an improvement of one full grade level. The only words he missed at the second-reader level were *quickly* for *quietly* and *careful* for *carefully*. At this time, he made no initial-sound errors and only one end-sound error. His mother reported that there were no more incidents of nausea, although Peter wasn't always happy to go to school. However, when it was time to go to the clinic, Peter never failed to remind his mother. While at the clinic, he particularly enjoyed the game activities. Twister was one of his favorite games.

Final Report of Fall Semester: The clinician reviewed initial digraphs and syllables and taught the endings of *ly*, *or*, and *er*. During this time, Peter kept a record of all the preprimer books and stories that he was able to read. During one of the sessions, the boy and his clinician spent time with the children's librarian. She showed Peter the shelves containing all the books and magazines for his reader level. Peter's mother reported that he insisted on going along whenever anyone in the family went to the library. She also said that he was able to read easily from simple books and children's magazines he brought home.

At the end of the fall session, he tested on the San Diego Quick Assessment at the high third-reader level. His only error on the third-grade list was a substitution of *strange* for *straight*. He knew this word was wrong but he didn't know how to correct it. All of the initial syllables of the words on the fourth-grade list were correctly pronounced; thus, Peter's total gain since first entering the clinic was three grade levels on the SDQA.

IV. Classroom-Reading Approach: Phonics Emphasized

Student: Maria R.	Age: 11	WISC Verbal	97
Grade	6	Performance	108
Actual Grade	6.6	Full Scale	103
WRAT (Reading)	7.0		
Difference	+.4		

Formula of Average Gain per Year

Average Gain per Year = AG
Actual Grade = Ac
WRAT Reading Score = WRS

$$\frac{AG}{Ac\,/\,WRS} \qquad \frac{1.06}{6.6\,/\,7.0}$$

In the sixth grade, Maria is slightly above average in sounding out words in isolation.

Problem: Inability to comprehend what she reads.

Gilmore Oral Comprehension: 3.15.

Mother's Report: "Maria got such a good start in a private school. My husband and I searched until we found a school with a strong phonics program. By Christmas of the first year, Maria could pick up magazines and newspapers and sound out many of the words. We've been very pleased with her ability to sound out words. However, she does not seem to understand what she reads. The teachers have been marking her low in comprehension ever since third grade. I don't see how she can pronounce the words and not know what she's reading, but she does."

Initial Interview: Maria is a beautiful girl. She is slender, has dark, brown eyes, and an olive complexion. She understands Spanish, although it is not often spoken in the home. She studies and carefully enunciates each word that she reads aloud. She said she doesn't like to read and she hates to do work sheets.

Initial Clinical Session: Maria said she had never really read a whole book. She said she chose books to report on that her friends told her about. Maria made the following substitutions on the San Diego Quick Assessment:

Grade Level	*Substitution*	*Stimulus Word*	*Error*
6	*a*ppáratus	apparatus	*a* as a schwa and accent on the wrong syllable
	gālléry	gallery	incorrect first syllable

Test Placement: On the SDQA, Maria can read at the sixth-grade level (words in isolation).

Error Analysis: Both words missed were phonetically defensible mispronunciations. Maria pronounced the "a" in apparatus as though it had the schwa sound of "a" in appellate. According to her teacher, whatever errors Maria makes are phonetically plausible errors.

Hypotheses to Be Tested:

1. Maria is so concerned with putting together sounds that she cannot progress much beyond the whole word.
2. Maria reads at a technical decoding level and gets no meaning from stories.

3. Maria does not enjoy reading; therefore, she avoids it and, consequently, is unable to improve.

Recommended Procedure:

1. Maria needs to have some fun associated with reading by playing reading games or engaging in game-like activities, such as:
   a. Do As I Say Cards
      Choose One Thing on a Card

Sing a note. Sing a line. Sing a song.

      etc.

   b. Follow room-mapping directions.
      Where would you be if you walked five steps east and six steps north? Etc.
   c. Follow directions to make Shake-a-Pudding.
   d. Follow directions for working magic tricks.
2. Bring in joke books and magazines appropriate for Maria's level and get her to anticipate the correct answer.
3. Have her read a city map and locate her school and her home.
4. Have her fill out catalog order blanks, listing items she would like to buy if she had $15 to spend.
5. Use reciprocal questioning at the sentence level, and later, at the paragraph level.
6. Flash phrases tachistoscopically.

Final Report of Spring Semester: Since we are not as much interested in Maria's word-attack skills as in her comprehension, we did not readminister the San Diego Quick Assessment. We did readminister the Gilmore Oral Reading Comprehension. She now tests 4.4, which is almost a year's growth in a single semester.

Maria's mother reports that she has been reading *Henry Huggins*[2] to her younger brother in grade four. She no longer reads at a slow pace.

Final Report of Fall Session: Maria is quite artistic. This semester she completed a neatly illustrated book on *Beverly Cleary and Her Books*. She had researched the life of the author and found many incidents interesting enough to serve as subjects for her illustrations. She started reading two additional books with the clinician's help and finished these at home.

---

[2]Beverly Cleary, *Henry Huggins* (New York: William Morrow and Co., 1950).

> Maria's ability to make up interpretative questions at sentence and paragraph levels has consistently improved.
>
> She has also learned to figure out the theme of the books she reads. She is beginning to enjoy reading books at the fourth-reader level.

In résumé, the cases presented represent four different classroom-reading approaches: individualized reading, use of basal readers, use of language experience, and emphasis on phonics. In all of the classrooms, some of the children learned to read without any difficulty, but it is also evident that in these same classrooms a few of them did not learn to read at all. These are the ones who required tutorial help. While it has often been said that there is no one best method to use in the classroom, there is, in fact, a best method for each individual child, and it is the complicated task of the teacher to discover this.

We know from first-grade research that a teacher who uses more than one method in her classroom increases her chances of reaching each child. The reason no single method is infallible is that children have different patterns of learning, as discussed in Chapter 1; therefore, the likelihood of reaching these children is increased with the addition of each new method. As in the cases cited, teachers and tutors do a better job of maintaining rapport, of tapping the child's interests, of beginning at an appropriate reading level, and of making reading profitable, than they do of taking time to discover the most effective learning pattern for each child. A reluctant reader may be unwilling to read, not because he can't, but because he does not choose to do so. For him the process of learning to read is unnecessarily boring because of the methods employed. He may already be able to read, but the classroom instruction is inappropriate for his particular pattern of learning.

11

REACHING BOYS

Obfuscated, bewildered boys are often plagued with admonitions such as: "Be still—don't poke your neighbor; sit up." Boys and fathers place a special value on physical activity; whereas girls, mothers, and teachers place a special value on sitting quietly.

In education today there is a tendency to ignore sex differences—boys, as well as girls, are expected to respond to the same educational stimuli with equal success. Educators, for some years, have stressed individual differences, while at the same time they have been blind to the differing educational needs of boys and girls—even though test scores have reflected sex differences, classroom practices in general have not. Classrooms have always been girl oriented. This is also true of recent experimentation with "open classrooms."[1] An "open classroom" refers to one in which the children select the daily curriculum. In this type of classroom, the reading curriculum, like the total curriculum, is whatever the child wants it to be. The boy who reads poorly never selects reading; therefore, it is nonexistent for him. Boys, as a group, are more prone to create chaos by making loud noises, scrapping, and testing behavior boundaries. Most boys cannot cope with curriculum changes which vary from highly structured to nonstructured. Girls tend to

[1] Herbert R. Kohl, *The Open Classroom* (New York: Vintage Books, Inc., 1969).

choose quiet curricular areas, such as reading, writing, clay modeling, and painting, and can adapt to curricular changes more readily than boys can. Girls are more likely to adjust to either the structured or the unstructured approach. In the traditional classroom, the reading program for the child with reading problems is likely to be too heavy. In the unstructured approach, a child with reading problems does not usually select reading, and, therefore, in both situations poor readers—particularly boys—are lost.

To identify a desirable classroom as having only an *open* or a *closed* curriculum is an anomaly. Within the same classroom there are individuals needing the security of a prescribed curriculum, and there are other individuals capable of making their own curricular decisions. This problem can be dealt with in different ways. The personnel of the University of California Laboratory School in Los Angeles[2] makes a concerted effort to match the child needing a high degree of structure with a teacher who provides this, and the child accustomed to decision-making with a more permissive teacher. A large elementary school system can provide for differences insofar as their staff can meet these needs.

The personnel in a small elementary school, however, strives to provide for the two extremes within every classroom. Both goals are lofty and difficult to achieve. In reading, a desirable program takes into consideration the two extremes: a prescribed curriculum, as in a developmental reading program, and a flexible curriculum, as in a self-selection program. Suggested student activities to implement a program of this latitude might be:

One child in the class—

1. Instructs another child in sounding out words that begin alike, as in *boy* and *big*.
2. Reads to another child in a different grade.
3. Helps another child read from a book (one already familiar to the child acting as teacher).
4. Reads directions to construct a model of some type.
5. Reads a library book of his choice.
6. Reads a magazine.
7. Reads a newspaper.
8. Reads a joke book.

---

[2]Madeline Hunter, "Orientation Speech Welcoming Visitors to the Los Angeles Laboratory School," University of California, Los Angeles, Oct. 1969.

Boys particularly benefit from activities of this kind that give them a chance to gain attention in a legitimate way. These daily choices may be increased and varied at the suggestion of the students in the class. The very act of a daily choice in all curriculum areas may be a relevant reading activity in itself.

Basically, reading is a nonboy-oriented activity. Education compounds the situation by emphasizing girl-oriented reading content, neatly written work sheets, routinely structured lessons, and inflexible grouping. This is particularly true in the primary grades. In recognition of these conditions, master teachers have used imaginative techniques to enliven their daily schedules and bombard boys with action-packed reading programs. These activities include error-free, enjoyable experiences, such as the following:

I. *Pantomime* (may be played with all initial consonants)

1. Place a large, yellow *B* on the board.
2. Draw a lower-case *b* inside the capital letter.
3. Sketch a *ball, bumblebee, boat, bird,* and *baseball bat* on the board.
4. A child is chosen to pantomime *one* of the activities suggested by the sketches, acting like a bumblebee or whichever action is indicated.
5. The child who correctly guesses the activity presented has the next turn.

(As long as the players stick to those words sketched on the board, the game is error free.)

II. *Bombs Away*

For this game, a windup toy bomb is needed which makes a loud noise after a minute or so. Any toy timer or interval timer could be used.

1. Build a collage made up of items beginning with *b*, such as *balloon, butter, bread, button, bottle,* or similar well-known words.
2. Wind the timer and hand it to the first student, who names any item from the collage. He then runs to the next student, hands the timer to him, and returns to his place. This boy, in turn, names a different item from the collection, and proceeds to pass the timer on to another student of his choice.
3. The object of this game is to name one of the words from the board before the timer goes off while it is in the possession of the student calling out the word.

III. *Drawing Relay*

1. This game is played with two teams of four students each.
2. At a signal, a member of each team runs to the board and quickly draws an article that can be found in the room starting with the same letter, such as *book, bookcase, baseball, bat, box,* and *blocks*. Each member of the team must draw a different item.
3. The team in which one of the members can correctly name all four items drawn by the opponents is declared the winner. If both teams are able to do this, results are a tie.

Activities for Boys Who Can Already Group Words That Begin Alike

I. *Paint a Word*

For this activity, a pail of water and a large paint brush are needed for each child.

1. Select a wide, outdoor cement sidewalk.
2. Each student writes his name on the sidewalk with wide sweeps of the wet brush.
3. Students are then asked to think of all the words they know beginning with a certain letter—say, *m*. They may mention words such as *moon, map,* and *Mother*.
4. At a given signal, students use their brushes and water to write as many words as they can beginning with this letter before their name dries.
5. The child receives credit for all recognizable words. This is not a spelling test; therefore, the teacher makes no effort to point out errors until the game is over.
6. The child competes with his own record or classmate of about the same level of ability.

II. *Word Baseball*

1. Five players are used in this activity, with positions as follows:

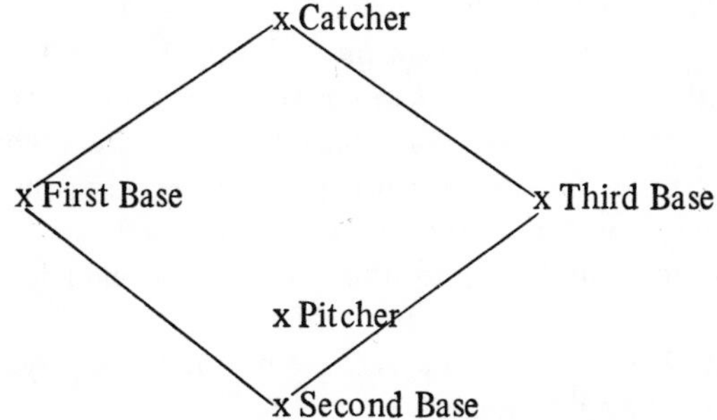

2. Three different sets of cards are used—one for each of the basemen—as follows: The first baseman has nouns written on his cards; the second baseman has verbs on his cards; the third baseman has cards containing adverbs. Complete sentences may be made with any combination of all three sets of cards.

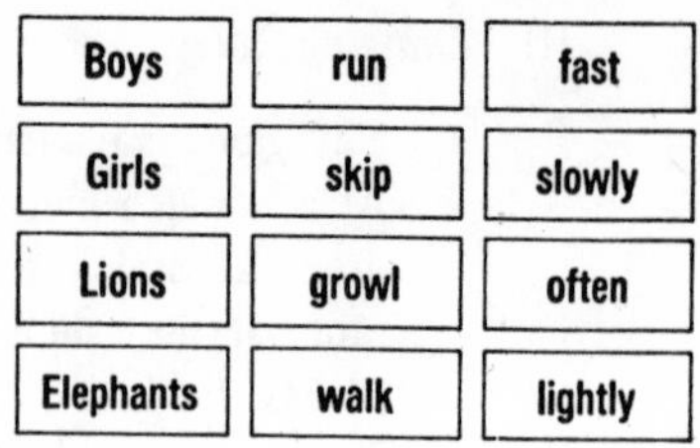

Boys
run
fast
Girls
skip
slowly
Lions
growl
often
Elephants
walk
lightly

3. The pitcher throws a ball to the catcher who catches it and runs to first base, where he has to identify the word held up by the first baseman before he can proceed to the next base. If unable to do this, the runner is told the word, tagged out, and replaced by the next player who steps up to the plate. Players, however, who successfully identify the word at first base continue to "run the bases" by correctly identifying each word as it turns up.
4. The aim of this game is to call out all three words flashed at each progressive base as quickly as possible, form a complete sentence, and score a home run for the individual.
5. When a student has successfully run the bases, he takes the place of the third baseman, and everyone moves up to the next place as the game continues.
6. The object of this game is to chalk up as many home runs as possible.

III. *Walk a Giant Step* (two players)

1. Players remove their shoes.
2. A stack of giant paper feet have been cut out from any kind of semi-heavy stock.

3. Four different words, known to the students, have been written on each of the giant feet and placed at intervals within stepping distance of each other.
4. One child begins to walk on each step, reading the word written on this step before proceeding to the next one. After successfully walking on all four giant steps, he may write a word of his own on a paper foot taken from a stack of paper forms and place this fifth step near the others on the floor.
5. The next child executes the same routine and adds his own word to the maze of footprints on the floor.
6. The object of this game is to see how far each player can progress before being "stumped."

IV. *Action Relay*

1. Two teams of four players each are chosen and a captain appointed for each respective team.
2. The captain stands a few feet away from his lineup of team members. He holds in his hands four cards with action verbs written in large print, such as *jump, skip, hop,* and *run*.
3. At a signal, the first person on each team reads the card held up by his captain and proceeds to approach the captain by carrying out the action indicated.
4. The first team to finish is declared the winner.

V. *Swami*

1. The teacher selects words standing for names of common items or objects beginning with the same letter or letter combination. She may then say: "I'll travel around the room with anyone who can read my mind. I plan to take with me a *block*, a *blazer*, and a *blanket*. Does anyone want to come with me?"
2. Children may guess, but they will not be invited to accompany her unless they catch on to the clue and call out a word that begins with *bl*.
3. As soon as a child guesses correctly, he joins hands with the teacher, repeating all previous words, plus his own word contribution.

   There are many variations of this game. One might be as follows: The teacher says, "I plan to take with me an *apple*, a *banana*, and a *cat*. Does anyone care to join me?"

   If further clues are needed, she may continue: "I will also take with me a *door* and an *elephant*." This may be continued through the alphabet, or as far as the group is able to go.

   Another variation might be based on the names of the boys in the class, the names of the girls, or Presidents of the country.

   This game, with its variations, may be effective for developing familiarity with word categories, phonics, word structures, synonyms, antonyms, and word-meaning skills. It may be especially appealing to bright boys who enjoy an exciting challenge.

Other Vocabulary-Building Activities

Directions for building models provide profitable reading practice for boys. Assembling precut wooden birdhouses, boats, and airplanes, according to written directions, results in a useful finished product plus the satisfaction of having worked independently. Directions for three-dimensional paper figures and airplanes can be found in *The Great International Paper Airplane Book.*[3] The completed paper planes flying around the classroom provide an added incentive for following directions carefully.

Games and do-it-yourself activities have the advantage of placing a value on the written word and making it a vital force in everyday living. Another technique which can be used daily, and for the same purpose, is a word bank. For the beginner, each new word learned is put on an index card. An accumulation of word cards can be counted, treasured, categorized, and worked with. The collection of cards—or *word bank*—can, for example, be taken to the "listening post." The following is a sample of teacher-made recordings that would help children to look at words in different ways:

Listening Post—Tape 1 (for use with word-bank cards)

"Hello, this is tape 1, page 1. Please write *1 dash 1* in the top right-hand corner of your page. Next, write your name in the top left-hand corner of your paper.

"While I hum, *Row, Row, Row Your Boat*, please place your word cards on the table, right side up. Ready now, listen—

"No. 1. If you can find the word *the*, write it near the top of your paper. If you cannot find *the*, write *NO—N–O*.

"No. 2. If you can find the name of an animal, copy his name underneath your first word. If you can't find the name of an animal, write *NO*.

"No. 3. If you can find a color, copy the name of the color underneath your other words. If you cannot find this, write *NO*.

"No. 4. If you can locate a word that tells about size, write this word on your paper. Size words are words like: *little, big, tall, short, fat,* or *skinny*. If you can't find a size word, write *NO*.

"No 5. If you can find any words that begin with the letter 'a,' list them on the paper underneath the other words. If you need more space, write on the back of your paper. If you get tired of writing words that begin with this letter, you might prefer drawing a picture of something that begins with *a*, like an airplane." (End of tape 1, page 1)

Tape 1, page 2 would include four new categories, and the fifth, then, would be to list words that begin with "*b*." Record as many of these on Tape 1 as you can—or better yet—ask for volunteers to record lessons in a similar manner so that other children can listen to peer recordings rather than to adult voices only.

---

[3]Jerry Mander, George Dippel, and Howard Gossage, *The Great International Paper Airplane Book* (New York: Simon & Schuster, 1967).

The idea of analyzing, preparing, and recording learning materials is difficult to initiate, but worth the effort. Boys should be encouraged to prepare tapes for their peers. In preparing to teach vocabulary or phonics to another child, the student-teacher has a reason to learn his own lesson well. First- and second-grade children, in the process of preparing such lessons, have asked for the teacher's manual, and with a little guidance have used this in a selective manner. When initiating such a program, it is well to let volunteers serve in the role of student in the instructor-learner relationship. This is a valuable experience for boys, even in the intermediate or upper grades. Contrary to expectations, they are not too blasé to enjoy the benefits of such relationships.

Another way of capitalizing on a boy's inherent interest is by sending secret messages in code or ciphers. A good source of information on the subject is *The First Book of Codes and Ciphers.*[4] Ciphers refer to a one-to-one relationship between letters and new symbols. Boys respond particularly well to a cipher involving numbers. Selection of a cipher using numerals often creates greater interest in reading for such boys. A simple introduction to ciphering would be to begin with the names of the boys. The following example is the name *Arthur* written in cipher. Tell the child with this name that the cipher represents the name of someone he knows better than anyone else in the world: *1, 18, 20, 8, 21, 18.*

1. The child notices the cipher contains six letters.
2. He notices that the second letter and the last letter are the same.
3. He knows that the person he knows best in the world is himself:

   1 = A   18 = R   20 = T   8 = H   21 = U   18 = R.

Next, write a simple sentence:

1, 18, 20, 8, 21, 18   23, 9, 14, 19   1   16, 18, 9, 26, 5.

1. The child recognizes the first word (Arthur), and also the third word (a).
2. At this point he is ready to write out the numbers and letters which he knows, to see if any certain pattern emerges:

   1 = A, 2 = B,__= C,__= D,__= E,__= F, 7 = G, 8 = H

In addition to the preceding activities involving gross motor movements, games, and teaching another child, a boy-oriented pro-

[4]Sam and Beryl Epstein, *The First Book of Codes and Ciphers* (New York: Franklin Watts, Inc., 1956).

gram needs to be relevant and functional. A student-written weekly newspaper or monthly magazine could serve such a purpose. A publication can provide the opportunity for a division of duties and an involvement of many persons in such positions as editor, proofreaders, reporters, ad men, printers, layout men, and illustrators. All of these positions will require reading and rereading articles and ads of varying levels of difficulty. The advertisements should be written for real services offered and actual items for sale. The events described should be of actual school functions that involve this particular grade or the entire school. Projects of this kind should extend over a semester or a year, depending on the children's success in producing the publication.

Silent Auctions also have appeal to boys who usually have an inborn love of "swapping." Functional reading and writing join many of the other educational experiences that contribute to this valuable and interesting activity. Since this is a "silent" auction, more writing and reading are involved than might at first be apparent.

1. The boy writes a permission slip—

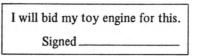

> Dear Mom,
>
> May I bring my______________
> to the Silent Auction to be held at
> _____etc.

2. He brings his toy or useful article to be auctioned at school, and places it on the auction table with a strip of paper containing his name, the name of the article, and a place for students to indicate their bids.
3. If a student sees an item that has appeal for him, he writes his name and bid on the accompanying piece of paper:

> I will bid my toy engine for this.
>
> Signed______________

4. On Friday, each child with an item on the auction table picks up his list of bids and draws a number.
5. The boy with number 1 can select whichever bid appeals to him from the list indicated on his sheet of paper, and he reads this aloud to the group. If the same bid occurs on other lists, students cross this item from their papers since it has already been taken.
6. It is possible that some items will have no appeal, and thus, no offers. These can be taken home or held over until the next auction, if the owner wishes to do so.

The Book Swap is similar to the preceding activity in that the boys take home permission slips. Books may be brought instead of toys or other items–but the books should be limited to paperbacks.[5] In certain instances, they may even include comic books. An important part of this campaign is the experience involved in the writing and reading of preliminary advertising material. A bulletin can be reserved for brief eye-catching ads, such as:

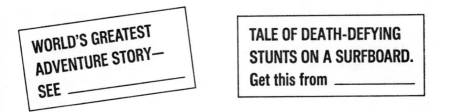

TALE OF DEATH-DEFYING
STUNTS ON A SURFBOARD.
Get this from ______

A boys' anthology is a cumulative effort that can sustain interest over a period of time. By a boys' anthology we mean a duplicated publication of the best of the boys' poems and stories, collected and judged from those submitted by the class over a period of time. These should be illustrated, and if possible, typed and duplicated by the students. Every boy should have at least one selection included in the publication, and after the books have been collated, each boy should read his own contribution into a tape recorder. These tapes can provide material that can be played by individuals or small groups at a listening post whenever they wish. In this way, the tapes and books can be enjoyed over and over again, and each child has the excitement of seeing his effort in print, plus hearing his own voice on the recorder.

Environmental reading can be used quite well to spark an interest

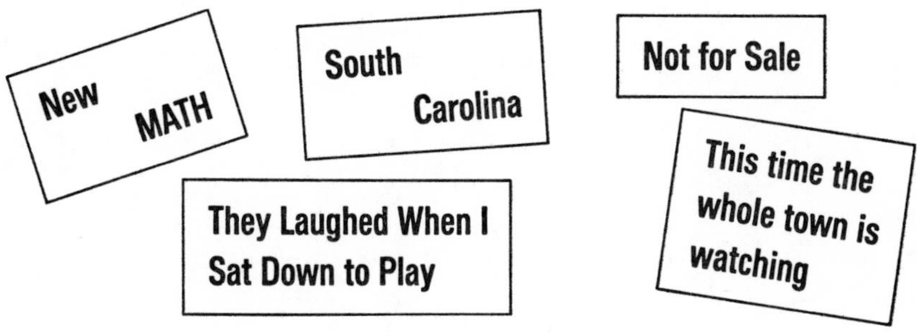

[5] See George Becker, " 'Off Beat' Paperbacks in Your Classroom," *Journal of Reading*, Nov. 1971.

in reading. This type of reading is apt to be relevant, available, and ongoing. Magazine ads, for example, can be cut and the captions mounted separately. (See captions at bottom of page 171.)
Next, ask the students to select one they can read or figure out with a little help. Following this, let them guess what is being advertised. In the above example, the New Math advertises a computer, and while the child is not likely to guess this, he will have done some constructive thinking about word meanings. All of the participants will become more and more aware of the reading involved in ads and the reading that surrounds them.

The same type of activity can be carried on using high-interest newspaper articles. Cut the headlines of appropriate articles and have the children select the one they can read. After they have made up a hypothetical sentence or paragraph, the teacher reads a paragraph which they attempt to match with the headlines they chose. Secondly, they compare the content they made up with the actual content.

Games and activities, such as those described above, constitute an effort to create a positive reading program slanted toward boys' natural instincts and interests. Games involving word recognition and manipulation, presented in a free and relaxed manner, can make reading pleasant and fun—and yet provide tools for students with which to forge solid skills. By making word activities a part of the daily lives of boys in school, learning to read soon becomes as natural for them as learning to speak.

12

READING WITH NONREADERS

The chapter title "Reading with Non-readers" is not paradoxical when the usual definition of reading is extended. Culturally devised codes, signs, and signals, such as skull and crossbones for poison, X for railroad crossings, and red flags for danger, are read with understanding even by those who cannot yet cope with the printed page. An understanding of the symbols that play a part in everyday living is taken for granted as a survival skill—yet this constitutes reading of an extended form. Our concern in this discussion is with those nonreaders of any age who may not have benefitted from traditional reading instruction.

Physicians and educators commonly call a severe reading disability "dyslexia." By severe, we mean an inability to respond to words and associate them with speech. For these students, even their own names are difficult to read. According to the medical profession, there is a tendency for congenital dyslexia to be carried by male members of the family more often than by female members. On this subject, which is of some concern to reading clinicians as well as physicians, the question is asked–Could congenital dyslexia be diagnosed as resulting from environmental factors as well as hereditary ones?

A cultural expectation for boys is that they develop physical prowess in team sports; for girls, that they learn quiet skills such as sewing and reading. Families often reinforce these expectations. The grandfather who says in front of his grandson, "I was the best guard on the basketball team, but I never did learn to read," is inadvertently setting a societal pattern for his grandson.

In surveying the literature for the past ten years, it is possible to find that definitions for "dyslexia" vary from "nonreader" to "one who reads two or more grade levels below his present grade."

In derivation, dyslexia comes to us from the Greek *lexicon* which means "words" and *dys* which means "difficulty." Students having difficulty with words are dyslexic, and beyond this, as we observed in the research reports, each researcher includes a more precise definition. The term dyslexia, without specific boundaries, is professionally not useful. For this reason, we use the term nonreaders to identify those with the capacity to read but with no record of achievement.

In a nonprofessional use, the term "dyslexia" serves two purposes well: first, it calls attention to those children experiencing difficulty in learning to read; second, it lends an air of respectability to their problem.

Every time an article on dyslexia appears in a magazine or newspaper, a large number of parents call the reading clinic and say, "My child is dyslexic. Is there anything you can do for him?" The fact that there is a label to pin on the child's lack of performance, and the fact that there are other children so afflicted–give a measure of comfort to the concerned parent. It reduces a feeling of guilt to be able to use an impressive label for a problem that the parent has not yet been able to solve. Insofar as the term dyslexia provides succor for the parent, it is useful. Parents with "so called" dyslexic children have very few sources of aid available to them.

One school designed to study dyslexic students aims to be so effective that it will eventually put itself out of business. The McGlannan School in Florida[1] admits only dyslexic children (congenital or acquired) and researches methods for reaching children who have not responded to conventional methods, such as basal readers, language experience, and individualized reading. The McGlannan School experiments with manipulative materials and multi-sensory input. Careful records are kept to document the techniques which work most successfully with a particular type of child. As the child is able to function in a normal situation, he is returned to public school. Detailed accounts are kept of procedures that have proven beneficial and these records are made available for public school use.

---

[1] Careth Ellingson and James Cass, "Teaching the Dyslexic Child: New Hope for Nonreaders," *Saturday Review*, 40 (April 1966), 82-85.

The Marianne Frostig Center of Educational Therapy at Los Angeles is also concerned with the child who is dyslexic. The widely used Frostig Test of Visual Perception[2] and Frostig Remedial Workbooks are an outgrowth of the work done in this research center.

Many other educators have been concerned with the neurologically dysfunctioning child. Notable among these are: Ebersole, Kephart, Orton, Cruickshank, and Delacato.[3] These dedicated authors have contributed much to education by suggesting methods effective for teaching some children, and by providing teachers with a variety of practical ideas. However, there is recurrent criticism of them with respect to meeting criteria of sound experimentation. Two of the most recent critical reviews are those of: Glass and Robbins,[4] and Reed, Rabe, and Mankinen.[5]

Never, well, hardly ever, is there a child for whom it is totally uneconomical to teach reading. The blind, the deaf, and the mute can be taught to enjoy reading. The educable mentally retarded child can learn to read well enough to become self-supporting. We have observed these children being taught to read in institutions, special schools, and even in our public schools. While teaching reading to these handicapped children seems costly, in the long run it is economical. Even those children classified by society as uneducable can become less dependent on others and lead fuller lives, upon gaining a basic knowledge of reading commensurate with their potential.

It is, therefore, of great importance to teach reading at some level to children not handicapped in hearing, sight, speech, or intelligence, but who have for some reason fallen far below their potential.

---

[2]Marianne Frostig, *Developmental Test of Visual Perception* (Palo Alto, Calif.: Consulting Psychologists Press, 1963).

[3]M. Ebersole, N. C. Kephart, and J. B. Ebersole, *Steps to Achievement for the Slow Learner* (Columbus, Ohio: Charles E. Merrill, 1968); N. C. Kephart, "The Needs of Teachers for Specialized Information on Perception," in W. M. Cruickshank (ed.), *The Teacher of Brain-Injured Children* (Syracuse, N. Y.: Syracuse University Press, 1966), pp. 169-180; J. L. Orton, "The Orton-Gillingham Approach," in J. Money (ed.), *The Disabled Reader* (Baltimore: Johns Hopkins Press, 1966), pp. 119-146; W. M. Cruickshank (ed.), *The Teacher of Brain-Injured Children: A Discussion for the Bases of Competency* (Syracuse, N. Y.: Syracuse University Press, 1966); C. Delacato, *Neurological Organization and Reading* (Springfield, Ill.: Charles C. Thomas, 1966).

[4]V. Glass and M. P. Robbins, "A Critique of Experiments on the Role of Neurological Organization in Reading Performance," *Reading Research Quarterly*, 10 (1965), 5-52.

[5]J. C. Reed, E. F. Rabe, and M. Mankinen, "Teaching Reading to Brain-Damaged Children: A Review," *Reading Research Quarterly*, 5 (1970), 379-401.

In reviewing clinical cases over the past ten years, children— no matter what their age—who entered the clinic as nonreaders, tended to have the following characteristics:

Impairment of—

visual perception
auditory perception
conceptualization
memory
motor coordination
control

Procedures were devised to deal directly with the inadequate responses resulting from these impairments.

VISUAL PERCEPTION

In treating impaired visual perception, the teacher asks that the child *watch* as a word is being written. The student follows movement and can, therefore, separate "field" from "ground." One of the symptoms of impaired visual perception is the child's tendency to begin reading at the end of the word, and consequently, reversing it—*saw* for *was*. By watching the word as it is being written, letter by letter, the child is compelled to view the word from the beginning. This teaching device also helps children overcome the tendency to enter a word in the middle and reassemble it incorrectly—*felt* for *left*.

AUDITORY PERCEPTION

When there is impairment of auditory perception, an introduction to reading which minimizes dependence on this particular sensory approach should be used. Introductions should be avoided which stress phoneme-to-grapheme relationships, as when you ask for /p/ as in pit or put, because this method builds on the child's weakest area. Those introductions are apt to be ineffective because they stress sound-to-symbol relationships. Methods which emphasize the visual and/or kinesthetic approach are good. A language-experience approach is appropriate if taught by a teacher sensitive to the auditory problem involved. This approach is most effective when vocabulary controls are built into the program. By asking for a word, which is presented visually by the teacher and then written by the child (and hopefully filed with other words having the same beginning), the child deals only with words that he has a need to use, and he can take his own time to abstract those which seem to have a similar beginning.

CONCEPTUALIZATION

To facilitate conceptualization of words, it is well to introduce them in a personal way. By combining a verb with a child's name—as in: *John, skip!*—you have a complete sentence and a direction that John can act out. The semantic boundaries of *skip* will begin to be defined by the child's own method of skipping. This may mean a half-skip, or a light double hop on the right foot and a single hop on the left foot—but to the child it has meaning. If he is asked to watch children skipping on the playground, he will understand what this involves. Eventually, since skipping is a developmental task, John may observe that kindergarten children have some difficulty in skipping, but that most second-grade children skip easily. By putting the word *skip* in the following word sets, the child will be helped to think of *skip* in terms of word structure, semantics, and syntax.

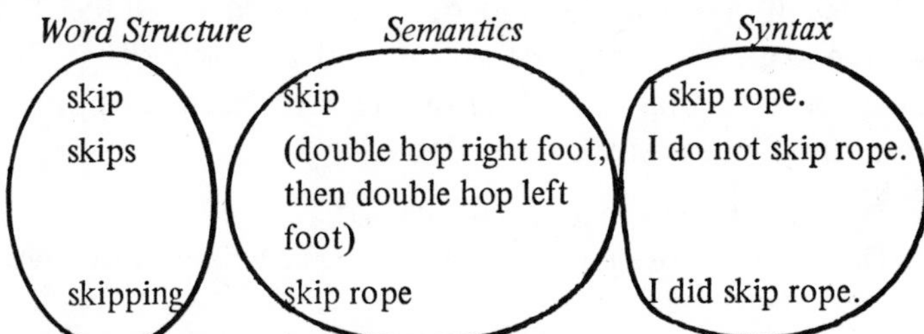

In general, conceptualization of a word may be explained as follows:

1. The word is presented as it applies to the child.
2. The word is used in a broader sense. In this example, it was used as it applied to other children in the classroom.
3. In an even broader sense, the word is applied to the next larger group. In this case it was applied to children on the playground.
4. The word must be categorized as to structure, semantics, and syntax.

MEMORY

To improve memory, it is possible to effect improvement in a retrieval system by building strong multi-sensory association with the thing to be remembered:

1. To introduce a word such as "heat," a hot plate or warm surface (such as a windowsill upon which the sun beats down) might be employed, to allow the child to feel the sensation of heat as he says and hears the word.
2. Encourage the child to draw an item or symbol that he feels will help him recall the word, and thus, an associative device may be forged that will assist the child. This symbol should be child-originated in order to be meaningful to him.
3. Practice immediate recall to test the effectiveness of the child's chosen symbol. If the symbol does not produce immediate recall, he should be encouraged to try another picture, sign, or code.
4. Test the word in a delayed-recall situation. Allow 30 minutes to elapse before testing the delayed recall, and be sure the test card includes the item drawn by the child to help him retrieve the word.
5. Ignore all incorrect responses and reward all correct ones. (It is exceedingly important when working with a child of this type *not* to show impatience with his attempts or with incorrect responses.)

Sylvia Ashton-Warner[6] suggests that learning is more likely to take place if there is a visceral involvement with the words chosen by the child, such as affection, love, hate, or fear. Grace Fernald[7] employs the same basic idea of a *felt* need by asking that the word introduced be one that the child *requests* to learn. In applying the Fernald method, these steps are followed:

1. The child requests to learn a word.
2. The word is spoken, and at the same time written with a heavy wax crayon, as the child watches.
3. The child says the word, hears it, and feels it as he traces over the heavy wax.
4. When the child feels secure enough to write the word, the model is removed from sight.
5. If the child cannot reproduce the word in its entirety, the steps are repeated until he is successful.

In both the Ashton-Warner and the Fernald techniques, the word is put into a simple sentence and filed for future use. Words collected in this manner become a part of the child's personal dictionary.

If none of the techniques so far discussed permit the child to retrieve the word, even at the immediate-recall level, a stronger input

---

[6] Sylvia Ashton-Warner, *Teacher* (New York: Simon & Schuster, 1963).

[7] Grace M. Fernald, *Remedial Technique in Basic School Subjects* (New York: McGraw-Hill, 1943).

system needs to be employed. Letters in clay, plastic, or heavy wood can be used. Then, as the word is learned, the thickness of the word model is diminished until, finally, the word is overlearned and can be written on a flat surface.

MOTOR COORDINATION

In working with faulty motor coordination, there are many activities listed in the Getman Manual[8] to improve eye-hand coordination. While total body coordination is of interest to us, for purposes of writing it is *essential* that eye-hand coordination be developed. For purposes of reading, there are many simple eye-movement exercises listed in this Getman Manual designed to improve binocular coordination at near point. In severe cases of faulty coordination at near point, the advice of an ophthalmologist should be sought.

CONTROL

Activities that help control the attention span need to employ some of the various attention-gaining devices, such as movement, sound, color, size, contrast, novelty, light, drama, exaggeration, and involvement. The effectiveness of most of these is well known, and all serve a purpose. Often, however, in severe cases, an innovative device is called for. It may be effective, with a highly distractable child, to provide an environment devoid of all outside influences such as those listed here, except as they may be centered solely on the word. Concentration, then, is more easily focused upon the particular word, which is written in bright colors, large size, contrasting shape, or in some manner that will capture the child's attention. The impact is great when all attention is concentrated on the word itself without any distracting exterior influences to vie for attention.

One of the reasons behind a child's short attention span may be that he has been operating in an area in which he has experienced nothing but failure. As most adults will agree, it is difficult to tolerate a situation in which one is completely outclassed in skill, speed, and knowledge. Reading clinics operate on the premise that all

---

[8]G. N. Getman and Elmer R. Kane, *The Physiology of Readiness* (Minneapolis: Programs to Accelerate School Success, Inc., 1964).

children need to experience some success *before* they can concentrate for periods of time in a productive manner.

A recent clinic case brought home this point. A third-grade boy was brought in with a learning disability so great that he had already been placed in a room for the educationally handicapped. This boy had average intelligence, but even in a small class or group his attention span was nil. His only interest in the clinic seemed to be to wander aimlessly about, or to race the small cars that other children had brought with them.

The two clinicians working with this boy found that the only letter he knew with any certainty was the first letter in his name. His name was the only word that he knew. They tried to use various alphabetic games to interest him, since he did not seem to recognize any of the words from readers that had been used in his grade at school. None of the games won any response from the youngster; nor did they interest him. The supervisor suggested that the clinicians present no more than five letters, beginning with those present in the boy's name. Then, if these were learned, they were to be combined with the youngster's name and a verb. This was done, and the boy became familiar with simple sentences. He was particularly interested in a booklet which was made by putting several pages of his work together. He was asked to make up illustrations for it, and this increased his interest. He read and reread the book to anyone who would listen. It was a source of great pride and pleasure to him to be able to read a "book." It was also a source of much satisfaction to the clinicians who had worked with the youngster to note the difference that had taken place in the attention span of this boy. The clinicians also noted that the boy no longer spent time aimlessly wandering around the room in search of toys and games.

Nonreaders, as a group, are not homogeneous. A wide range of variations is found within this category. Each student has a different pattern of ability but most have some of the following prereading skills:

1. Can place pictures in sequence.
2. Can distinguish circles, squares, and other geometric forms.
3. Can find letters that look alike.
4. Can read the codes, signs, and signals in the environment.
5. Can read his own name if written in one way; i.e., manuscript.
6. Can read his name if printed or written in either upper- or lower-case letters.

7. Can spell his name (not that spelling is important here, but the familiarity with letters is important).
8. Can match words that look alike.

Any nonreader who has all eight of the above skills can probably be taught to read in tutoring sessions, and in a short time feel more comfortable in his regular classroom than he was before. The smaller the number of these abilities present and the older the student, the less favorable is the prognosis for his learning to read.

Through early diagnosis and application of appropriate methods, children identified as nonreaders in this chapter may be aided to reach their potential through the efforts of a sensitive and knowledgeable teacher. The percentage of nonreaders in the population, although small, constitutes an important segment. Educators have an obligation to recognize the worth of each individual and employ appropriate measures to develop each child to the fullest.

APPENDICES

I	Informal Tests
II	Basic Skills Records
III	High Interest, Low Vocabulary Books
IV	Exploring Multi-Media Aids

Appendix I

Informal Tests

All of the following tests can be duplicated by the teacher. Oral directions are included in Chapter 1 for the Reading Readiness Test, Parts I and II, and for the Pattern of Learning Test.

Part I: Letters

Aa Bb Cc Dd Ee Ff
Gg Hh Ii Jj Kk Ll
Mm Nn Oo Pp Qq Rr
Ss Tt Uu Vv Ww Xx
Yy Zz

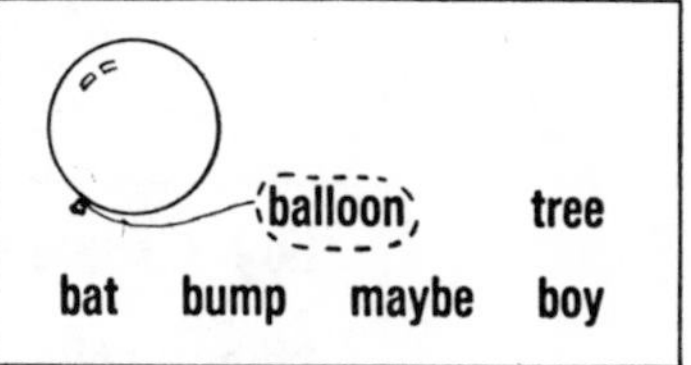

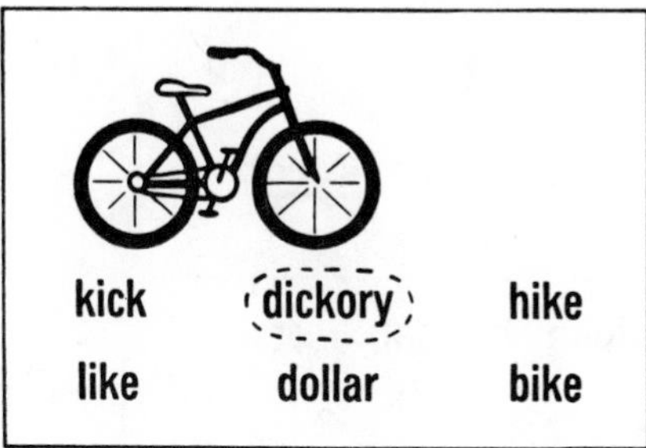

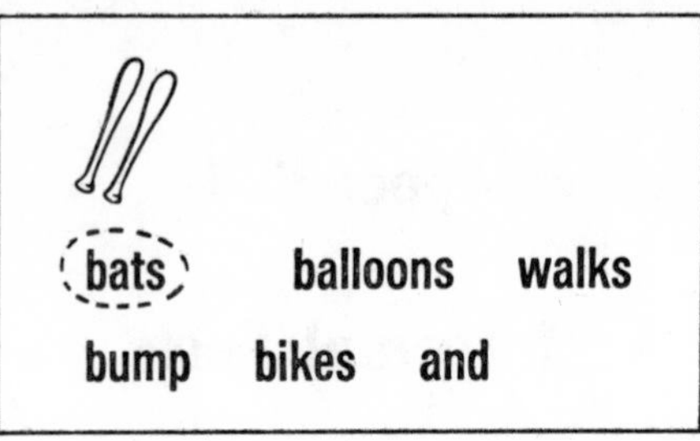

danger great bottle
silly kite umbrella

B C A
a b c

W Y P
p y w

Z K G
g z k

R S T
s t r

boy something goes
bikes likes hikes

Part II: Words

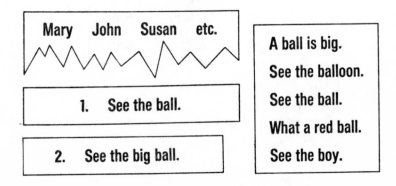

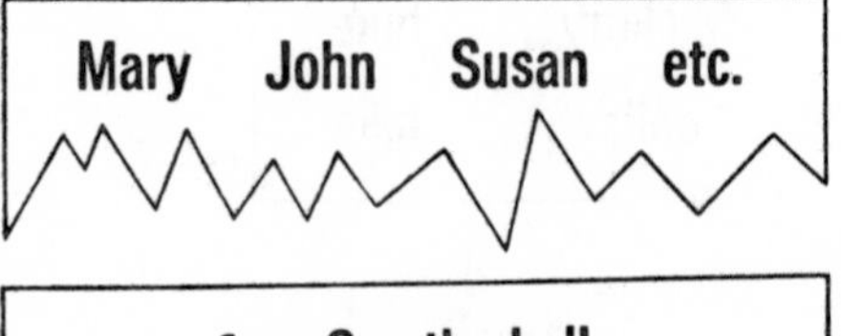

1. See the ball.

2. See the big ball.

A ball is big.
See the balloon.
See the ball.
What a red ball.
See the boy.

PATTERN OF LEARNING TEST

Review Sheets

Directions for the Pattern of Learning Test can be found in Chapter 1 on pages 32-33.

The review sheets to be used at the end of each of the four teaching periods are copied below.

Review set to be used after teaching Set I.

Review set to be used after teaching Set II.

Review set to be used after teaching Set III.

These papers are to reinforce the correct response, which is told to the child if necessary, and therefore the papers are not scored.

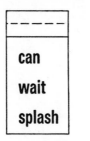

PATTERN OF LEARNING TEST

Group Tests

These same tests can be used on Friday in periods II, III, and IV, and on Monday morning as group tests.

** TEST FOR SET I **

		SCORE Circle One
can	big can cat an at man can can can an	(PA) 0 25 50 75 100
wait	wait said we meat wait card sound wait wait want	(MA) 0 25 50 75 100
splash	splash splint splash on dash cash splash mash sash splash	(SA) 0 25 50 75 100

** TEST FOR SET II **

		SCORE Circle One
Circle *long* every time you see it.	song it long long wing long get to gnat long	(MA) 0 25 50 75 100
Circle *pin* every time you see it.	nap pin not put pin pat pin man pin is	(SA) 0 25 50 75 100
Circle *bride* every time you see it.	bride big side kite ride bump bride bride ride bride	(PA) 0 25 50 75 100

** TEST FOR SET III **

		SCORE Circle One
rope	dip rope road pit rope hope rope deep rope and	0 25 50 75 100 (SA)
match	hatch chat match match mat match match chair little latch	0 25 50 75 100 (PA)
jar	camp bar carry see jar can jar jar jar cat	0 25 50 75 100 (MA)

SAN DIEGO QUICK ASSESSMENT

(Pronunciation Test)

Directions for administering this test are found in Chapter 3 on pages 62 and 64.

RR[1] *Matching Level (Alike or different)*		*RR*[2] *Reading Readiness Level (Letter names)*	*PP*	*Primer*	*1*
B	B	B	see	you	road
A	C	A	play	come	live
M	M	M	me	not	thank
C	C	C	at	with	when
S	Q	S	run	jump	bigger
J	J	J	go	help	how
T	T	T	and	is	always
H	H	H	look	work	night
D	L	D	can	are	spring
W	M	W	here	this	today

2	*3*	*4*	*5*	*6*
our	city	decided	scanty	bridge
please	middle	served	business	commercial
myself	moment	amazed	develop	abolish
town	frightened	silent	considered	trucker
early	exclaimed	wrecked	discussed	apparatus
send	several	improved	behaved	elementary
wide	lonely	certainly	splendid	comment
believe	drew	entered	acquainted	necessity
quietly	since	realized	escaped	gallery
carefully	straight	interrupted	grim	relativity

7	*8*	*9*	*10*	*11*
amber	capacious	conscientious	zany	galore
dominion	limitation	isolation	jerkin	rotunda
sundry	pretext	molecule	nausea	capitalism
capillary	intrigue	ritual	gratuitous	prevaricate
impetuous	delusion	momentous	linear	risible
blight	immaculate	vulnerable	inept	exonerate
wrest	ascent	kinship	legality	superannuate
enumerate	acrid	conservatism	aspen	luxuriate
daunted	binocular	jaunty	amnesty	piebald
condescend	embankment	inventive	barometer	crunch

PREPRIMER STARTER LIST

This list of words is common to most of the present day preprimers. Children familiar with these words should be able to read independently at the preprimer level.

a	here	little	something
and	I	me	the
can	in	my	to
down	is	not	up
go	like	play	with
		see	you

SAN DIEGO GRADED OPPOSITES

Refer to Chapter 3 for the use of this test.

Primer Words

Teacher says:		*Child reads silently and selects:*
Sample	walk	go (run) see
	1. dislikes	likes jump look
	2. stand	see was sit
	3. down	you at up
	4. little	boy big bad
	5. out	in its is
	6. came	was went were
	7. unhappy	happy house have
	8. went	candy car came

FIRST LEVEL

Sample: throw — call / car / (catch)

1. girls	bump	boys	baby
2. slower	faster	seesaw	hop
3. man	pole	window	woman
4. pick up	drop	step	bear

5. hers	foot	his	rain
6. can	never	catch	cannot
7. lost	button	found	jingle
8. night	give	across	day

Sample: night — (day) / dark / down — SECOND LEVEL

1. square	rosy	round	read
2. last	fist	fast	first
3. left	red	right	round
4. dark	light	low	leave
5. noisy	still	stand	silly
6. close	oven	over	open
7. back	from	front	free
8. fearless	after	over	afraid

Sample: heavy — dark / (light) / black — THIRD LEVEL

1. good-bye	hello	help	hold
2. rough	gone	garage	gentle
3. soft	had	head	hard
4. serious	squeal	silly	jeep
5. asleep	awake	away	always
6. east	with	west	word
7. more	less	lead	load
8. sat	said	stood	was

Sample: north — east / said / (south) — FOURTH LEVEL

1. remember	fierce	ferry	forget
2. roughly	stride	smoothly	slope
3. false	trial	throb	true
4. queen	king	kept	kite
5. shy	bold	bad	burn
6. most	level	least	ledge
7. yours	maybe	me	mine
8. unable	able	art	after

Sample: fat — slow / (slender) / spew

FIFTH LEVEL

1. real	flat	fake	tough
2. exit	scout	ancient	entrance
3. outer	inner	flow	ramps
4. weak	folks	model	strong
5. dried	soaked	scoop	hedge
6. wonderful	details	awful	awkward
7. indirect	firm	queer	direct
8. incorrect	correct	witness	praised

TEST
SAN DIEGO WORD MEANINGS

PRIMER

Teacher reads:

The teacher reads the stimulus word only, in the primer list. The remaining words in the test are read silently.

Directions: "Circle the word in the box at the right that best defines or fits the word which I read."

Teacher reads			
Example: *A* a brother	boat	(boy)	house
1. animal	dog	boat	ball
2. a home	like	something	house
3. food	to eat	to play	to sing
4. toy	down	with	doll
5. not big	little	like	to
6. something round	my	box	ball
7. a color	red	I	here
8. a sister	and	fat	girl

FIRST

Directions: Read the sample aloud, making sure students understand what they are to do and circle correct word in the example.

Example: *A* Jane	a boy	a bat	(a girl)
1. a woman	a father	a mother	a brother

2. a color	road	back	black
3. a place to live	a town	a book	a bug
4. an animal	a tree	a goat	a boat
5. not big	huge	small	large
6. something that flies	kite	street	tree
7. something to eat	sandwich	rock	paper
8. something with which to play	table	rug	bicycle

SECOND

Directions: Read the sample aloud, making sure students understand what they are to do and circle correct word in the example.

Example: *A* something to drink is	sand	white	(water)
1. white and shiny	black	clean	dirty
2. milk	to drink	to color	to cut
3. at night, turn on a	fight	kite	light
4. a sore	hurts	talks	sees
5. a knife	walks	cuts	cats
6. a stove	cold	hat	hot
7. a house	to live in	to burn up	to cut up
8. one who lives near	an enemy	a night	a neighbor

THIRD

Directions: Read the sample aloud, making sure students understand what they are to do and circle correct word in the example.

Example: *A* a book is something	to sew	(to read)	to wash
1. seven and one	eight	late	ate
2. a bat and ball go	apart	together	never
3. summer sun	cold	freezing	warm
4. winter ice	soft	milk	frozen
5. a dark color	white	black	pink
6. color of the sun	blue	brown	yellow
7. fast	quickly	slowly	not at all
8. lion's roaring	frightening	soothing	gentle

FOURTH

Directions: Read the sample aloud, making sure students understand what they are to do and circle correct word in the example.

Example: *A* a joke is something	to cry about	(to laugh at)	to be bored with
1. a friend is someone you	hate	like	avoid
2. a magician can do	magic	muddling	nothing
3. a boat is for	traveling on water	sinking	breaking
4. a car is for	tipping	wrecking	driving

5. a road is for	riding on	sleeping on	camping on
6. when there is no noise there is	silence	chaos	cacophony
7. a person who talks when someone else is talking	lectures	is polite	interrupts
8. a person born in a country is	a native	a foreigner	a car

FIFTH

Directions: Read the sample aloud, making sure students understand what they are to do and circle correct word in the example.

Example: *A* someone you've just met is	an old friend	an enemy	(an acquaintance)
1. someone from another country is	a foreigner	a friend	a neighbor
2. every state in the United States has a	car factory	capitol	lake
3. two people who disagree are likely to	argue	cry	be happy
4. to think over an idea is to	cancel it	consider it	cash it
5. to buy and sell things is a	brother	bother	business
6. a difficult task can be a	challenge	charger	bottle
7. a topic to talk about will be	discussed	dismantled	disarmed

8. U.S. Congress	law making justice law enforcing

SIXTH

	Directions: Read the sample aloud, making sure students understand what they are to do and circle correct word in the example.
Example: *A* the paraphernalia that you work with is your	(apparatus) ground pattern
1. artwork is displayed in an Art	gallows gallon gallery
2. grades 1 through 6 are considered	secondary elementary primary
3. stating what you think	comment withdraw question
4. laughable	ridiculous ridden raddled
5. a palace is likely to be	mousy malevolent magnificent
6. a business street is	communal commercial uncommon
7. to put an end to is to	refute continue abolish
8. to inquire is to	question answer deny

MODIFIED CLOZE TEST

Directions

Ask the children to read the appropriate level paragraph silently and fill in the blanks with words from those listed in the box below the paragraph. In reader levels primer through grade four, picture clues help the children to get ready to read.

PRIMER

fish

The children looked at __________ fat fish. He was __________, very big. "Can a __________ ride on the fish's __________?" a little boy asked. "__________," said his dad. "We __________ see him do this."

ride	can	man	big	back	yes	the

FIRST

lions

Five lions walked into __________ cage. They looked big __________ bold. The man walked __________ the cage a minute __________ the lions. He looked __________ and scared. Then he __________ a gun. Now the __________ looked scared.

little	opened	after	into	and	lions	the	shot

SECOND

bicycle

The boy rode his __________ with one hand. He __________ to do tricks. Once __________ did not watch carefully __________ he ran over a __________. His bicycle almost __________ over. After that he __________ using both hands.

rock	tipped	rode	liked	car	and	bicycle	he

THIRD

Watermelon

Fortunately, for those who__________watermelon but dislike the __________, a seedless watermelon has__________grown. It is smaller__________the usual watermelon. It__________also more expensive. Lazy__________will appreciate not having__________ spit out the seeds.

to	been	than	is	seeds	like	eaters	go

FOURTH

Elephants

Elephants are large animals,__________would you believe that __________are even larger? Did__________know that whales are __________too? A baby whale__________weigh more than two__________. And that is no__________story.

whales	but	fish	you	can	elephants	mammals

FIFTH

Map of Thailand

THAILAND
Bangkok

Children in Thailand are__________to respect their parents. __________may want to go__________a celebration but if dad says no, they__________they cannot go. Even__________ they are disappointed, they__________expected to hide this.

are	their	they	taught	know	though	to	do

SIXTH

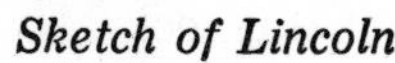

Sketch of Lincoln

Lincoln learned a great __________ about how to write __________ picking a well-written article __________ omitting appropriate and well-chosen __________. He would copy the __________ of the article but __________ blank spaces where the __________ words had been. Weeks __________ he would attempt to __________ in the missing words.

---

and fill deal later well-chosen left by words remainder

SAN DIEGO QUICK ORAL INVENTORY

Refer to Chapter 3 for the use of this test

PP	The boy looked at a toy. The toy is a big red airplane. I like red airplanes. I can be happy.	3	Mike got wonderful presents. Finally only one huge box remained. "It will be your favorite gift," his friend suggested excitedly.
1	How sad the boy is now. His toy boat cannot be found. Mother said, "Ask for a new one for your birthday."	4	Jim studies the universe. "You mean the stars are suns? Then are other planets orbiting them?" he asked in disbelief.
2^1	Pat woke up. He walked to school. No one was at school. "This is not a school day," said Pat.		
2^2	Bob walked into the big house. Suddenly, "Surprise!" shouted all the neighbors. "We waited for you to have a party."		

SAN DIEGO INFORMAL SILENT INVENTORY

2. Ann got a very big box for her birthday.
"I wish I could see through it," she said.
"Open it," her mother said. "It has something you can ride on."

1. What did Ann get?
2. How do you know that Ann didn't know what was in the box?
3. What did her mother ask her to do?
4. What do you think was in it?
A dog, a doll, a bicycle?

3. One planet known to have life is the earth.
Some think that the planet Mars could have life, too, so science-fiction writers have written about what Martians would be like. What wild ideas they have!

1. What planet has life on it?
2. What was said to make you think that Mars has life?
3. What do science-fiction authors write about?
4. Which one might be the description of a Martian:
A white man 5′ 6″ tall, a green man 3′ tall,
a black man 6′ tall?

4. The tiger is a big jungle cat found in Asia. He grows to a weight of 500 pounds and over, and he is a vicious hunter.
Tigers are flesh eating and dangerous.

1. The tiger belongs to what animal family?
2. Describe the tiger in two ways.
3. How does a tiger's weight compare with yours?
4. Tigers will eat: wild berries, other animals, underbrush.

5. The peace-loving Crow Indians owned large herds of horses in the 1800's, but they suffered losses in wars with the Blackfoot and Sioux. Because of this, they sought to be friends with the early settlers.

1. The Crow Indians had large numbers of what?
2. What kind of warriors were they?
3. What kind of warriors were the Blackfoot and Sioux?
4. They became friends with the early settlers:
   to get protection, to sell furs, to sell horses.

SAN DIEGO GRADED PARAGRAPH TEST

Read the graded paragraph to the right and mark it in the three following ways:

1. Put 1 in front of the first sentence that tells you what the paragraph is about.
2. Put *S* in front of the sentences that tell you more about the sentence with a 1 in front of it.
3. Put an *R* in front of the sentence that reviews what the other sentences tell you or restates one of the ideas.

2

City mice are wise. Early each night I set a trap with cheese. Late each night I hear mice nibbling. Early each morning I see the cheese is eaten. Late each morning I see the mice running free. I think the mice are wiser than me.

3

A fence always needs attention. Sometimes it needs paint. Loose boards need to be nailed back. Gates fall off the hinges. A neighbor's goat cracks a board. How can you be lazy on a summer day when you have fence work to do?

4

Your life history is being made right now. What you do is not likely to change the course of the government, but it will set the course of your life. You can determine now whether you will be agreeable and happy, or critical and unhappy. The history of your life is what you make it.

5

A large prehistoric animal which had a monstrous shape was a stegosaurus. This animal had a small lizard-like head with a brain the size of a peach. Great plates of bone grew in double rows along each side of the spinal cord. It could be said that the stegosaurus had bulk, brawn, and very little brain.

Appendix II

Basic Skills Records

SAN DIEGO CHECKLIST OF BASIC SKILLS

Student ________________________________ Actual Grade __________

Grade Level __________

Words in Isolation	*San Diego Quick Assessment* (Pronunciation)	__________
Meaning of Words	*San Diego Word Opposites*	__________
	San Diego Word Meanings	__________
Reading in Context	*Informal Oral Inventory*	__________
	Informal Silent Inventory	__________

Phonics and Structure Skills	*Check Known*	*Fill in with dates:* *Began Work on*	*Completed*
1. Can match 10 letters quickly (See SDQA)	______	____________	________
2. Can name 8 out of 26 letters (See SDQA)	______	____________	________
3. Knows 8 initial consonant sounds (Circle: b c d f g h j k l m n p r s t v w z) (See Phonics Sheet A)	______	____________	________
4. Correctly reads words with s, ed, ing (See Phonics Sheet B)	______	____________	________
5. Knows 10 words on the Preprimer Starter List	______	____________	________

Phonics and Structure Skills	*Check Known*	*Fill in with dates:* *Began Work on*	*Completed*
6. Can identify end consonants correctly (See Phonics Sheet B)	______	____________	________
7. Can identify medial consonants correctly (bi*gg*er wi*ll*ing ma*k*ing)	______	____________	________
8. Can figure out new words from context clues:	______	____________	________
—picture clues	______	____________	________
—initial sounds	______	____________	________
—medial sounds	______	____________	________
—end sounds (See Phonics Sheets A and B)	______	____________	________
9. Knows the letters in order (A B _ D _ _ G _ I, etc.)	______	____________	________
10. Can locate a word in a dictionary	______	____________	________
11. Can combine two known words to make a new compound word. (dog/house) (See Sheet C)	______	____________	________
12. Can figure out new words beginning with digraphs wh, th, ch, and sh (See Phonics Sheet A)	______	____________	________
13. Knows when *c* sounds like *s* (cent, city), when followed by *i* and *e*; sounds like *k* at other times (See Sheet C)	______	____________	________
14. Knows the *l* consonant clusters, as *bl, cl, fl, gl, pl, sl* (See Phonics Sheet A)	______	____________	________

Phonics and Structure Skills	*Check Known*	*Fill in with dates:* *Began Work on*	*Completed*
15. Knows the *r* consonant clusters, as *br, cr, dr, fr, gr, pr, tr* (See Phonics Sheet A)	______	__________	______
16. Knows the following consonant clusters: *sp, st, sn, sm, sc, scr*	______	__________	______
17. Knows the rhyming ending of a — ay at e — ew et i — in ite o — og op u — ug un	______	__________	______
18. Knows medial vowel changes, as *bat, bet, bit, bot, but* (See Phonics Sheet A)	______	__________	______
19. Knows one-syllable words ending in *e* cap cape pet Pete kit kite rot rote cut cute	______	__________	______
20. Knows the division of words, as:			
a. vc/cv den/tist mot/to (See Phonics Sheet C)	______	__________	______
b. v/cv o/bey de/ny (See Phonics Sheet C)	______	__________	______
c. /*cle* a/ble lit/tle (See Phonics Sheet C)	______	__________	______
Vocabulary Building			
1. How to read diacritical marks (key words)	______	__________	______
2. Practice in locating words by 2nd and 3rd letters	______	__________	______

Phonics and Structure Skills	*Check Known*	*Fill in with dates: Began Work on*	*Completed*
3. Prefixes *re, un, bi*	______	____________	______
4. Suffixes	______	____________	______
er, or	one who, agent	teacher, tutor	
al, ial	related to	educational, tutorial	
ment	act of doing	government	
5. Root words	______	____________	______
actum	to act, do, arouse, to set in action	agent, act, action, actual, active, actor	
factum	to do, make	factory, factor fashion, factual	
lectum	choose, collect, gather	elect, re-elect select, lecturer	
scriptum	to write	script, manuscript transcript inscription	
statum	to stand, remain	statue, stationary station	
6. Finding synonyms	______	____________	______
7. Finding antonyms	______	____________	______
8. Finding homonyms	______	____________	______
9. Finding homographs	______	____________	______
10. Test of word opposites	______	____________	______
11. Test of words defined	______	____________	______
12. Using the dictionary to check multiple meaning	______	____________	______
Words in Phrases and Sentences			
1. Phrase marking	______	____________	______
2. Phrase reading	______	____________	______
3. Phrase memory	______	____________	______
4. Reading dialogue	______	____________	______
5. Cloze Test	______	____________	______
6. R/Q of sentences	______	____________	______
Paragraph Analysis			
1. First sentence which tells most	______	____________	______

Phonics and Structure Skills	*Check Known*	*Fill in with dates: Began Work on*	*Completed*
2. Supporting sentences	______	______	______
3. Summary sentence (San Diego Graded Paragraph Test)	______	______	______
4. Important words put in telegram form	______	______	______
5. Literal meaning	______	______	______
6. Interpretive meaning	______	______	______
7. Applied levels	______	______	______
8. R/Q of paragraphs	______	______	______

Content Analysis			
1. Setting	______	______	______
2. Character	______	______	______
3. Point of view	______	______	______
4. Problem or content	______	______	______
5. Resolution or ending	______	______	______
6. Theme	______	______	______
7. Style	______	______	______
8. Bias	______	______	______
9. Figures of speech—*Common*			
a. metaphor *The sky is a blue umbrella.*	______	______	______
b. simile The blue sky is *like* a huge umbrella.	______	______	______
c. personification The blue sky is friendly and smiles down at us.	______	______	______
d. analogy Even as the car requires water, gas, and oil, to run well, the human body requires vitamins, calories, and protein.	______	______	______
e. euphemism (Death is reported as—) He *passed on.*	______	______	______

Phonics and Structure Skills	*Check Known*	*Fill in with dates: Began Work on*	*Completed*
10. Figures of speech—*Uncommon*	______	______	______

a. metonymy: one word which stands for the name of what is meant
The pen (literature) is mightier than the sword (force).

______ ______ ______

b. onomatopoeia: A word which sounds like the action or object for which it stands
"The *tintinnabulation* that so musically wells/From the bells." (Edgar Allan Poe)

______ ______ ______

c. allegory: a story with a symbolic meaning

______ ______ ______

d. parable: a symbolic short story to answer a single question

e. antithesis: direct opposite
To err is human; to forgive, divine.

______ ______ ______

f. hyperbole: exaggeration, such as "a thousand pardons"

______ ______ ______

g. epigram: (1) an inscription, (2) a short poem with a sting, (3) any pungent saying, (4) a style full of such sayings

______ ______ ______

h. apostrophe: words to a present or absent person or thing and breaking the thread of discourse

______ ______ ______

i. synecdoche: (part for a whole) *He hired 500 hands. (persons)* (or whole for a part) *He ate of the tree. (fruit)*

______ ______ ______

SAN DIEGO READING PROFILE

Student ______________________ Date ______________

	Word Pronunciation	Word Meaning		Content Comprehension			
Grades	WRAT READING	S D Graded Word Meaning	S D Graded Word Opposites	S D Cloze Test	S D Informal Oral Inventory	S D Informal Silent Inventory	S D Graded Word Paragraphs
Above + 3							
+ 2							
+1							
Actual + Grade	+1 −1						
Below 1							
2							
3							
4							

SAN DIEGO ANALYSIS OF ERRORS SHEET

ame of the student ______________________ Age_____ Birthday______________
mo. day year

hool ______________________ Grade_______ Teacher______________
Elem. Jr. High Sr. High

ttitude toward reading: ______________________________________

____

ttitude during test(s): ______________________________________

____

TESTS

ISC			*WIDE RANGE ACHIEVEMENT*—I or II
ate ________	________		Date ________
A. ________	________		Reading (word pronunciation) ________
erbal IQ ________	________		Arithmetic ________
rformance IQ ________	________		Spelling ________
ull-Scale IQ ________	________		Examiner ________
xaminer ________	________		*SAN DIEGO QUICK ASSESSMENT* ____

ERROR ANALYSIS

oring key:	Position of Error	Type of Error	
	(1) initial	(1) reversal	(5) long vowel
	(2) medial	(2) consonant	(6) phonogram
	(3) final	(3) consonant blend	(7) prefixes
		(4) short vowel	(8) suffixes
			(9) root word
			(10) miscellaneous

Stimulus Word	Substitution	Position	Type	Similarly Patterned Words

Word Attack Skills Needed:

SHEET A–PHONICS RECORD
Initial Consonants
Short Vowels
Digraphs
Initial Consonant Clusters

Color Code:
Nov.–black
Feb.–green
May–red

MATCHING
LOCATING
TOTAL RECALL

	1. b c f h t	2. a e i o u	3. p m j k s	4. d l g r w	5. z y qu n v	6. wh sh ch th	7. bl cl fl gl pl sl	8. br cr fr gr pr tr
KEY WORDS NAMES	bat cat fat hat tat	bat bet bit bot but	pumps mumps jumps kit sit	dig lag gig rig wig	zip yip quip nip van	whip ship chip that	blot clot flat glad plot slot	brag crack from grit prim trim

SHEET B—PHONICS RECORD
Consonant Endings
Inflected Endings
Long-Vowel Sounds

	1. b t p m k	2. s d l g r	3. z v n sh	4. ch th ng	5. s ed ing	6. ly ful fully	7. er	8. a e i o u
KEY WORDS	tab tat tap tam tack	kiss bed bell beg beggar	buzz love fin fish	catch with wing	helps helped helping	lovely helpful careful helpfully carefully	catcher buzzer fisher helper backer	cake Pete kite hope cute
NAMES								

SHEET C—WORD ATTACK SKILLS

Small Letter c (k / s)

Compound words

vc/cv

v/cv

/cle

	y = i	y = ē	c = s	c = k	compound words	vc/cv	v/cv	/cle
KEY WORDS	cry	lady	city	cat	doghouse	dentist	obey	able
	dry	Tommy	cent	cot	lookout	pencil	silent	cradle
	fry	kindly	citizen	cut	seesaw	walnut	divide	table
	pry	windy	certain	clash	boxcar	swallow	travel	marble
	try	city		crash	cowboy	mustard	minus	stable
	wry	busy			newsboy	doctor	gravy	purple
NAMES								

SHEET D—WORD ATTACK SKILLS

Root words
Prefixes
Suffixes

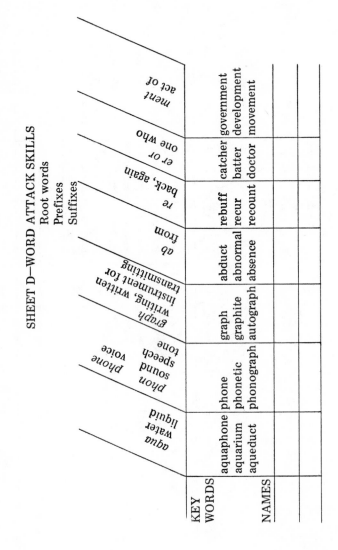

	aqua water liquid	*phon* sound speech tone *phone* voice	*graph* writing, written instrument for transmitting	*ab* from	*re* back, again	*er* or one who	*ment* act of
KEY WORDS	aquaphone aquarium aqueduct	phone phonetic phonograph	graph graphite autograph	abduct abnormal absence	rebuff recur recount	catcher batter doctor	government development movement
NAMES							

AN INVENTORY OF READING ATTITUDE

(Standardization Edition)

Name______________________________Grade________Boy Girl
Last First Middle

School___________________________Teacher__________________

Date of Test ______________________
Mo. Day Yr.

TO BOYS AND GIRLS:

This sheet has some questions about reading which can be answered YES or NO. Your answers will show what you usually think about reading. After each question is read to you, circle your answer.

INSTRUCTIONS TO PUPILS

Draw a circle around the word YES or NO, whichever shows your answer.

Sample A

Yes No Do you like to read?

If you like to read, you should have drawn a circle around the word YES in Sample A; if you do not like to read, you should have drawn a circle around the word NO.

Sample B

Yes No Do you read as well as you would like to?

If you read as well as you would like to, you should have drawn a circle around the word YES in Sample B; if not, you should have drawn a circle around the word NO.

Yes No 1. Do you like to read before you go to bed?
Yes No 2. Do you think that you are a poor reader?
Yes No 3. Are you interested in what other people read?

Yes	No	4.	Do you like to read when your mother and dad are reading?
Yes	No	5.	Is reading your favorite subject at school?
Yes	No	6.	If you could do anything you wanted to do, would reading be one of the things you would choose to do?
Yes	No	7.	Do you think that you are a good reader for your age?
Yes	No	8.	Do you like to read catalogs?
Yes	No	9.	Do you think that most things are more fun than reading?
Yes	No	10.	Do you like to read aloud for other children at school?
Yes	No	11.	Do you think reading recipes is fun?
Yes	No	12.	Do you like to tell stories?
Yes	No	13.	Do you like to read the newspaper?
Yes	No	14.	Do you like to read all kinds of books at school?
Yes	No	15.	Do you like to answer questions about things you have read?
Yes	No	16.	Do you think it is a waste of time to make rhymes with words?
Yes	No	17.	Do you like to talk about books you have read?
Yes	No	18.	Does reading make you feel good?
Yes	No	19.	Do you feel that reading time is the best part of the school day?
Yes	No	20.	Do you find it hard to write about what you have read?
Yes	No	21.	Would you like to have more books to read?
Yes	No	22.	Do you like to read hard books?
Yes	No	23.	Do you think that there are many beautiful words in poems?
Yes	No	24.	Do you like to act out stories that you have read in books?
Yes	No	25.	Do you like to take reading tests?

Supt. of Schools, Dept. of Educ.
San Diego County 5-65

INDIVIDUAL READING ATTITUDE ASSESSMENT

Name ______________________________ Date ______________
yr. mo. day

School ______________________ Grade ____ Birth-date ____________

Age ______________
yr. mo.

Introduction: "Look at the picture at the bottom of this page. Has anyone ever asked you—'Would you like a single- or a double-dip ice-cream cone?' If you were the child in this picture, which one of these answers would be the one you would say—('I'd like a single; I'd like a double; I don't care.')?"

TAKE TIME TO FIND OUT WHY THE CHILD ANSWERS AS HE DOES. DISCUSS FLAVORS OR, IN THE EVENT HE DISLIKES ICE-CREAM, TALK ABOUT SOME OF HIS FAVORITE FOODS. WHILE THIS ITEM IS NOT SCORED, IT IS IMPORTANT THAT THE CHILD UNDERSTAND THAT HE SHOULD TRY TO CHOOSE THE ANSWER MOST SIMILAR TO THE ONE THAT HE WOULD MAKE. IF NONE OF THE ANSWERS IS SIMILAR, THE CHILD SHOULD FEEL FREE TO MAKE UP HIS OWN.

PART OF THE EFFORTS OF THE EXAMINER SHOULD BE DEVOTED TO PROBING FOR FOODS WHICH THE CHILD DISLIKES. THE CHILD SHOULD BE MADE TO FEEL FREE TO EXPRESS HIS FEELINGS WITHOUT FEAR OF CENSORSHIP. SOME FOODS WHICH CHILDREN COMMONLY DISLIKE ARE EGGS, ONIONS, SPINACH, AND SALADS.

"There are 12 more pictures. Let's see if we can figure out what you would say if you were the child in the picture. Remember, if none of the answers sound like what you'd say—you can make up your own." (Be sure to encourage the child to give you the *first* response that comes to his mind.)

You can only take out one book.
Why not more?
How come?
Who cares?
1.

What would you like?
A game.
I don't care.
The book.
2.

What are you doing?
Nothing much.
I have to read a book.
Reading a good book.
3.

Where are you going?
To the show.
No place special.
To the library.
4.

What are you reading?
A library book.
I'm looking at pictures
A comic book.
5.

We just went past your stop.
It could never happen to me.
That's just like me.
Oh well--
6.

Would you like to go biking?
I'd rather watch T.V.
Yes, I'll bike.
I'd rather read.
7.

What mark did you get in reading?
A good one.
A bad one.
So-so.
8.

How can we find the answer?
Ask someone.
Look in a book.
Guess.
9.

Who would like to read a story to some young children?
Not me.
I would.
It'd be okay, I guess.

After supper would you read to me?
Do I have to?
From an easy book?
That sounds like fun.

Working a puzzle.
Reading a book.
Going to sleep.
What are you doing?
12.

ATTITUDE ASSESSMENT SCORE SHEET

STUDENT________________ ACTUAL GRADE_______ READING LEVEL_______

1. + Why not more?________
   o How come?________
   – Who cares?________

2. – A game.________
   o I don't care.________
   + The book.________

3. o Nothing much.________
   – I *have* to read a book.____
   + Reading a good book.____

4. – To the show.________
   o No place special.________
   + To the library.________

5. + A library book.________
   – I'm looking at pictures.____
   o A comic book.________

6. – It could never happen to me.________
   + That's just like me.________
   o Oh well - -.________

7. o I'd rather watch T.V.________
   – Yes, I'll bike.________
   + I'd rather read.________

8. + A good one ________
   – A bad one.________
   o So-so.________

9. o Ask someone.________
   + Look in a book.________
   – Guess.________

10. – Not me.________
    + I would.________
    o It'd be okay, I guess.________

11. – Do I have to?________
    o From an easy book?________
    + That sounds like fun.________

12. – Working a puzzle.________
    + Reading a book.________
    o Going to sleep.________

TOTAL ATTITUDE SCORE
Positive ________
Negative ________

Add the total positive scores and subtract the minus -- (5 neutral scores equal one minus score).

Appendix III

High Interest, Low Vocabulary Books[1]

The following high-interest, low-vocabulary, annotated list contains books particularly appropriate for use with remedial readers or with those readers who are capable but unmotivated.

Agle, Nan H. *Three Boys and H_2O.* Scribner's, 1968.

Reading Level: grade 4
Interest Level: grades 3-6

The Triplet boys and their Grandmother visit the seashore with a student of Oceanography. There is much information about the sea woven into the story.

Three Boys and a Helicopter, 1958.
Three Boys and a Lighthouse, 1951.
Three Boys and a Mine, 1954.
Three Boys and a Train, 1956.
Three Boys and a Tugboat, 1953.
Three Boys and Space, 1962.
Three Boys and the Remarkable Cow, 1952.

All About Books. Random House, 1953-62.

Reading Level: grades 4-6
Interest Level: grades 4-8

Some titles are *All About:*

Andrews	*Dinosaurs*
Andrews	*Strange Beasts of the Past*
Andrews	*Whales*
Goodwin	*Rockets and Space Flight*
Henry	*Horses*
Lemmon	*Monkeys*
Lemmon	*Strange Beasts of the Present*
Sperry	*The Jungle*

[1] This list is presented through the courtesy of the Superintendent of schools, Department of Education, San Diego County, California. Compiled mainly by members of the staff of the School Library Services, the list appears here with minor modifications.

American Adventure Series. Emmet A. Betts, ed. Row-Peterson, 1941-1965.

Anderson	*Comanche and His Captain*
Anderson	*Friday, the Arapaho Indian*
Anderson	*Portugee Phillips and the Fighting Sioux*
Anderson	*Squanto and the Pilgrims*

Reading Level: grade 2

Anderson	*Alec Majors*
Anderson	*Pilot Jack Knight*
Beals	*Chief Black Hawk*

Reading Level: grade 3

Anderson	*Grant Marsh, Steamboat Captain*
Beals	*Kit Carson*
Coombs	*Alaska Bush Pilot*
Garst	*Cowboys and Cattle Trails*
Tucker	*Dan Morgan, Rifleman*

Reading Level: grade 4

Anderson	*Wild Bill Hickok*
Beals	*Buffalo Bill*
Beals	*Davy Crockett*
Coombs	*Rocket Pioneer*
Coombs	*Sabre Jet Ace*

Reading Level: grade 5

Andersen, Hans C. *Flying Trunk*, translated by Lyda Jensen. Scott, Foresman, 1951.

Reading Level: grade 3
Interest Level: grades 3-7

Twenty-four well-loved fairy tales.

Anderson, Clarence W. *Billy and Blaze*. Macmillan, 1936.

Reading Level: grade 3
Interest Level: grades 2-5

A horse-loving boy and his pony, Blaze, have adventures which are continued in *Blaze and the Gypsies, Blaze and Thunderbolt, Blaze and the Mountain Lion, Blaze Finds the Trail, Blaze and the Forest Fire, Blaze and the Indian Cave,* and *Blaze Shows the Way.*

Aulaire, Ingri d' and Parin d'. *Benjamin Franklin*. Doubleday, 1950.

Reading Level: grade 4
Interest Level: grades 4-8

An easy, colorful tale of this popular character. Also useful are the authors' *Abraham Lincoln* and *Pocohantas.*

Beim, Jerrold. *Country Garage*. Morrow, 1952.

Reading Level: grade 2
Interest Level: grades 3-5

Seth proves his ability to help his uncle at the filling station.

Bialk, Elisa. *Tizz*. Children's Press, 1955.

Reading Level: grade 3
Interest Level: grades 2-5

This is the first of a long series of books about the pony, Tizz. All are easy, printed in large type, and popular.

Books to Begin On. Holt, Rinehart and Winston, 1959-1970.

Simple vocabulary, large type, and high interest level distinguish these books that are not written for beginning readers but are written as an introduction to a field of interest that is new to the reader.

Clymer, Eleanor	*Wheels* 1965
de Borhegyi, Suzanne	*Museums* 1962
Fenton, Sophia H.	*Greece* 1968
Hill, Elizabeth S.	*Bells* 1970
Holsaert, Eunice and Faith	*Ocean Wonders* 1965
Phelan, Mary Kay	*The Circus* 1963
	The White House 1962
Sebastian, Lee	*Rivers* 1966
	The South Pole 1968
Softly, Barbara	*Magic People* 1967
	Magic People Around the World 1970
Swenson, Juliet M.	*Hawaii* 1962
Table, Gladys	*Flower Arranging* 1969
Tina, Dorothy Less	*Alaska* 1962
Waller, Leslie	*American Invention* 1963
	The American West 1966
	Clothing 1969
	Electricity 1968
	Numbers 1960
	Our American Language 1961
	Our Flag 1960

Buff, Mary and Conrad. *Dash and Dart*. Viking, 1942.

Reading Level: grade 3
Interest Level: grades 3-5

The story of two baby fawns and their life in the forest.

Bulla, Clyde R. *Sword in the Tree*. Crowell, 1956.

Reading Level: grade 3
Interest Level: grades 3-8

An adventure story of the days of King Arthur. Also useful by the same author are *Old Charlie; Riding the Pony Express; Squanto, Friend of the White Men;* and *John Billington, Friend of Squanto.*

Burger, Melvin. *Stars*. Coward, 1971.

Reading Level: grade 1
Interest Level: grades 2-3

Atoms and space distance have been introduced to primary children through televised moon explorations. This attractive book discusses these difficult topics in a manner that will interest primary children.

Burton, Virginia Lee.*Calico the Wonder Horse*. Houghton, 1950.

Reading Level: grade 4
Interest Level: grades 4-8

A comic-book-type Western. *Mike Mulligan and His Steam Shovel*, easier to read, is also popular for intermediate grades and for reading to primary children.

Carmer, Elizabeth and Carl. *Captain Abner and Henry Q*. Garrard, 1965.

Reading Level: grade 3
Interest Level: grades 2-5

An American tall tale of ageless appeal. Another of the same type by these authors is *Mike Fink and the Big Turkey Shoot.*

Cavanah, Frances. *Our Country's Story*. Rev. ed., Rand, 1962.

Reading Level: grades 3-4
Interest Level: grades 3-7

An easy introduction to American history.

Cerf, Bennett. *Book of Riddles*. Random, 1960.

Reading Level: grades 1-2
Interest Level: grades 1-8

A "Beginner Book" with a single riddle on one page and the answer on the back of the page. Simple cartoon-like illustrations. Followed by *More Riddles* by same author.

Chandler, Edna W. *Cowboy Sam Books*. Beckley Cardy, 1951-1960.

	Reading Level	*Interest Level*
Cowboy Sam and Big Bill	Preprimer	Preprimer-gr. 2
Cowboy Sam and Freckles	Preprimer	Preprimer-gr. 2
Cowboy Sam and Dandy	Preprimer	Preprimer-gr. 2

Cowboy Sam and Miss Lily	Primer	Primer-gr. 3
Cowboy Sam and Porky	Primer 1	Primer-gr. 3
Cowboy Sam	Primer 2	Primer-gr. 3
Cowboy Sam and Flop	Gr. 1	Grs. 1-4
Cowboy Sam and Shorty	1	1-4
Cowboy Sam and Freddy	1	1-4
Cowboy Sam and Sally	2	2-5
Cowbov Sam and the Fair	2	2-5
Cowboy Sam and the Rodeo	2	2-5
Cowboy Sam and the Airplane	3	3-6
Cowboy Sam and the Indians	3	3-6
Cowboy Sam and the Rustlers	3	3-6

A very popular series of readers about a cowboy and his adventures. Cartoon-type illustrations.

Chandler, Edna W. *Native American Series.* Benefic, 1956-1963.

	Reading Level	Interest Level
Taka and His Dog	Gr. 1	Grs. 1-3
Kala's Pet	1	1-3
Juanito Makes a Drum	1	1-3
Tall Boy and the Coyote	1	1-5
Little Cedar's Tooth	2	2-6
Buffalo Boy	2	2-6
Little Wolf and the Thunder Stick	3	3-6

Easy and exciting stories of American Indians.

Childhood of Famous Americans Series. Rev. ed., Bobbs, 1959-1961.

Reading Level: grades 3-4
Interest Level: grades 4-8

Guthridge	*Tom Edison*
Snow	*Sequoyah*
Stevenson	*Abe Lincoln*
Stevenson	*Buffalo Bill*
Stevenson	*George Carver*
Stevenson	*George Washington*
Stevenson	*Virginia Dare*
Stevenson	*Wilbur and Orville Wright*
Van Riper	*Babe Ruth*
Van Riper	*Lou Gehrig*

Simple biographies which are popular with children. There are many other similar titles in this series.

Christopher, Matt. *Catch That Pass!* Little, 1969.

Reading Level: grades 3-4
Interest Level: grades 3-7

For the football fans. Other easy sports stories by this author are *Break for the Basket, Touchdown for Tommy, Tall Man in the Pivot, Long Stretch at First Base,* and *Hard Drive to Short.*

Cleary, Beverly. *Runaway Ralph.* Morrow, 1970.

Reading Level: grades 3-4
Interest Level: grades 3-6

A hilarious sequel to *The Mouse and the Motorcycle.* Ralph runs away to camp with unexpected results. The author's *Ellen Tebbits* and *Henry Huggins* are also fun.

Coleman, James C. *Deep-Sea Adventure Series.* Harr Wagner, 1962.

	Reading Level	Interest Level
Sea Hunt	Gr. 2	Grs. 4-9
Treasure Under the Sea	2	4-9
Submarine Reserve	3	4-9
Pearl Divers	3	4-9
Frogmen in Action	3	4-9
Danger Below	4	4-9
Whale Hunt	4	4-9
Rocket Divers	5	5-9

Cordts, Anna D. *Tommy O'Toole Books.* Benefic, 1957-1958.

	Reading Level	Interest Level
Tommy O'Toole and Larry	Gr. 1	Grs. 1-4
Tommy O'Toole at the Fair	2	2-5
Tommy O'Toole and the Forest Fire	3	3-5

Adventure tales of a young Irish railroad man.

Corson, Hazel W. *Air-Age Books.* Benefic, 1955-1964.

	Reading Level	Interest Level
Peter, the Rocket Sitter	Gr. 1	Grs. 1-4
Peter and the Rocket Fishing Trip	1	1-4
Peter and the Rocket Team	2	2-5
Peter and the Big Balloon	2	2-5
Peter and the Unlucky Rocket	2	2-5
Peter and the Rocket Ship	3	3-6
Peter and the Two-Hour Moon	3	3-6
Peter and the Moon Trip	3	3-6

Exciting stories of Peter's trips into space. In some classes, the teacher might read this to the children.

Dalgliesh, Alice. *Fourth of July Story*. Scribner, 1956.

Reading Level: grade 4
Interest Level: grades 4-7

A simple introduction to our best-known patriotic holiday. By the same author: *Thanksgiving Story* and *Columbus Story*. Good for reading aloud to whole class.

Daugherty, James H. *Andy and the Lion.* Viking, 1938.

Reading Level: grade 3
Interest Level: grades 3-7

A modern version of Androcles and the Lion. Amusing comic-book-type drawings.

Dennis, Wesley. *Flip*. Viking, 1941.

Reading Level: grades 2-3
Interest Level: grades 2-6

A horse story with full-page illustrations, accompanied by not more than six lines of text in large type. Other titles: *Flip and the Cows* and *Flip and the Morning.*

Derman, Sarah. *Big Top.* Benefic, 1958.

Reading Level: primer
Interest Level: primer to grade 2

Clem, a water boy in the circus, teaches Dell, an elephant, to do tricks.

Derman, Sarah. *Monkey Island*. Benefic, 1957.

Reading Level: grade 1
Interest Level: grades 1-3

The monkeys in the park select a new king.

Derman, Sarah. *Poker Dog.* Benefic, 1958.

Reading Level: grade 1
Interest Level: grades 1-3

Poker dog wins a home after many adventures.

Derman, Sarah. *Pony Ring.* Benefic, 1957.

Reading Level: primer
Interest Level: grades 1-3

Andy trains the pony, Rusty, to share and behave in the riding ring.

Derman, Sarah. *Pretty Bird*. Benefic, 1957.

Reading Level: preprimer
Interest Level: preprimer-grade 2

A parakeet adjusts to a new home and the other pets of the household.

Derman, Sarah. *Surprise Egg.* Benefic, 1958.

Reading Level: preprimer
Interest Level: preprimer-grade 2

Little hen hatches an egg which does not belong to her.

Discovery Books. Garrard, 1960-1965.

Reading Level: grades 3-4
Interest Level: grades 2-8

Beach	*Theodore Roosevelt*
Berry	*Leif the Lucky*
Carmer	*Francis Marion*
Carmer	*Henry Hudson*
Colver	*Abraham Lincoln*
Colver	*Florence Nightingale*
Davison	*Buffalo Bill*
Epstein	*George Washington Carver*
Graff	*John Paul Jones*
Graves	*Annie Oakley*
Graves	*Benjamin Franklin*
Kaufman	*Thomas Alva Edison*
Latham	*Sam Houston*
Parlin	*Amelia Earhart*
Patterson	*Frederick Douglass*
Rose	*Clara Barton*
Wilkie	*Daniel Boone*

Authentic biographies with appeal for young readers. Other similar titles are available in this series.

Dolch, Edward W. *Basic Vocabulary Series.* Garrard.

Reading Level: grade 2
Interest Level: grades 1-6

Animal Stories (1952)
Bear Stories (1957)
Circus Stories (1956)
Dog Stories (1954)
Elephant Stories (1956)
Folk Stories (1952)
Horse Stories (1958)
Irish Stories (1958)
Lion and Tiger Stories (1957)
Lodge Stories (1957)
More Dog Stories (1962)
Navaho Stories (1957)

Pueblo Stories (1956)
Teepee Stories (1956)
"Why" Stories (1952)
Wigwam Stories (1956)

Written with Dolch 220 basic sight words and 95 commonest nouns.

Dolch, Edward W. *First Reading Books.* Garrard.

Reading Level: grade 1
Interest Level: grades 1-4

Big, Bigger, Biggest (1959)
Dog Pals (1959)
Friendly Birds (1959)
I Like Cats (1959)
In the Woods (1958)
Monkey Friends (1958)
On the Farm (1958)
Once There Was a Bear (1962)
Once There Was a Cat (1961)
Once There Was a Dog (1962)
Once There Was an Elephant (1962)
Once There Was a Monkey (1962)
Once There Was a Rabbit (1961)
Some Are Small (1959)
Tommy's Pets (1958)
Zoo Is Home (1958)

Written in the easier half of 220 basic sight words and 95 commonest nouns.

Dolch, Edward W. *Folklore of the World.* Garrard.

Reading Level: grade 3
Interest Level: grades 2-8

Stories from Alaska (1961)
Stories from Canada (1964)
Stories from France (1963)
Stories from Hawaii (1960)
Stories from India (1961)
Stories from Italy (1962)
Stories from Japan (1960)
Stories from Mexico (1960)
Stories from Old China (1964)
Stories from Old Egypt (1964)
Stories from Old Russia (1963)
Stories from Spain (1962)

Written from the Dolch "Storyteller's Vocabulary" of 684 words.

Dolch, Edward W. *Pleasure Reading Books.* Garrard.

Reading Level: grade 3
Interest Level: grades 3-8

Aesop's Stories (1951)
Andersen Stories (1956)
Fairy Stories (1950)
Famous Stories (1955)
Far East Stories (1953)
Greek Stories (1955)
Gulliver's Stories (1960)
Old World Stories (1952)
Robin Hood Stories (1957)

Rewritten with first thousand words for children's reading.

Estep, Irene. *Pioneer Series.* Benefic, 1957-1959.

Reading Level: grade 4
Interest Level: grades 4-8

Pioneer Pilgrim
Pioneer Buckaroo
Pioneer Tenderfoot
Pioneer Engineer

Stories of pioneer life and activities in various sections of our country.

Faulkner, Georgene. *Hidden Silver.* Scott, Foresman, 1952.

Reading Level: grade 3
Interest Level: grades 4-8

An entertaining story of how Sally hides the family silver from the King's soldiers during the Revolutionary War. Girls will like this.

Fenner, Phyllis. *More Stories for Fun and Adventure.* Day, 1964.

Reading Level: grades 4-5
Interest Level: grades 4-8

A collection of short, humorous stories. Follows *Stories for Fun and Adventure.*

Fletcher, Sydney E. *Big Book of Cowboys.* Grosset, 1964.

Reading Level: grades 3-4
Interest Level: grades 3-8

Big colorful pictures showing cowboy togs and paraphernalia. Very popular. The text is not easy but the pictures make this useful at all levels.

Freedom Series. Bowmar, 1971.

These books are relevant; they are sure to fire the avid reader and even spark the interest of reluctant readers.

I Am Freedom's Child

Freedom's Apple Tree
America I Know You
It's America for Me
Spoiled Tomatoes
Poor Old Uncle Sam
Adam's Balm
Once There Were Bluebirds
I Reach Out to the Morning
Gentle, Gentle, Thursday

Geisel, Theodor S. *Cat in the Hat.* Random, 1957.

Reading Level: grade 2
Interest Level: grades 2-4

Nonsense from Dr. Seuss. Most of the Dr. Seuss titles have ageless appeal and reading level is for grades 2-4. A sequel is *Cat in the Hat Comes Back.*

Green, Carla. *I Want to Be ---- Series.* Children's Press, 1957-1961.

Reading Level: grades 2-3
Interest Level: grades 2-6

Easy vocational material about bus drivers (P.629.2), mechanics (P.621), farmers (P.630), carpenters (P.694), fishermen (P.639.2), storekeepers (P.641.4), etc.

Harris, Louise D. *Slim Green.* Little, 1955.

Reading Level: grade 4
Interest Level: grades 4-8

Habits and characteristics of snakes. Teacher might read at intermediate level.

Hays, Wilma. *Cape Cod Adventure.* Coward-McMann, 1964.

Reading Level: grades 4-5
Interest Level: grades 4-7

Buried treasure, robbers, and an island make an exciting story with a Cape Cod setting. *The Scarlet Badge* by the same author is also useful.

Haywood, Carolyn. *Eddie the Dog Holder.* Morrow, 1966.

Reading Level: grades 3-5
Interest Level: grades 3-6

Humorous episodes about Eddie and his dog holding business. *Eddie and Gardenia, Little Eddie,* and *Eddie's Pay Dirt* by the same author are equally well liked.

Heffernan, Helen and others. *Desert Treasure.* Harr Wagner, 1955.

Reading Level: grade 4
Interest Level: grades 6-9

A story of adventure and the Mojave Desert.

Heffernan, Helen and others. *Mysterious Swamp Rider.* Harr Wagner, 1955.

Reading Level: grades 4-5
Interest Level: grades 5-8

An adventure about the Revolutionary War. Originally published as *The Adventures of Canolles.*

Henderson, Le Grand. *How Basketball Began.* Abingdon, 1962.

Reading Level: grade 4
Interest Level: any age

A humorous tale about how basketball began. Another similar title: *How Space Rockets Began.*

Henry, Marguerite. *The Little Fellow.* Holt, Rinehart and Winston, 1945.

Reading Level: grade 2
Interest Level: grades 1-4

Story of an appealing little colt who overcomes his jealousy and finds happiness. Slight text and full-page illustrations.

Hoff, Syd. *Thunderhoof.* Harper, 1971.

Reading Level: grade 1
Interest Level: grades 2-3

As usual Hoff's illustrations reflect the humor in the story line.

Hogner, Dorothy C. *Earthworms.* Crowell, 1953.

Reading Level: grade 3
Interest Level: grades 3-8

Habits and characteristics of earthworms. See also *Spiders* and *Butterflies* by the same author.

How They Lived Series. Garrard, 1967-1969.

Reading Level: grade 4
Interest Level: grades 3-6

Blassingame	*Bent's Fort*
James	*When Men Panned Gold in the Klondike*
McCague	*When Cowboys Rode the Chisholm Trail*
Patterson	*Lumberjacks of the North Woods*

Exciting tales of dramatic episodes in American history. Other titles in this series are equally useful.

Huber, M. B. and others. *Wonder-Story Books.* Row-Peterson, 1953.

Interest Level: to grade 8

It Must Be Magic—Book 4
They Were Brave and Bold—Book 5
These Are the Tales They Tell—Book 6

Old favorite stories attractively illustrated.

Hurley, William J. *Dan Frontier Series.* Benefic, 1959-1963.

	Reading Level	*Interest Level*
Dan Frontier	Preprimer	Preprimer-grade 2
Dan Frontier and the New House	Preprimer	Preprimer-grade 2
Dan Frontier and the Big Cat	Primer	Primer-grade 3
Dan Frontier goes Hunting	Primer	Primer-grade 3
Dan Frontier, Trapper	Gr. 1	Grs. 1-4
Dan Frontier and the Indians	1	1-4
Dan Frontier and the Wagon Train	2	2-5
Dan Frontier Scouts with the Army	2	2-5
Dan Frontier, Sheriff	3	3-6
Dan Frontier Goes Exploring	3	3-6

Indians Series. Garrard, 1965-1969

Reading Level: grade 3
Interest Level: grades 2-5

Blassingame	*Sacagawea*
Graff	*Squanto*
Meadowcroft	*Crazy Horse*
Montgomery	*Chief Seattle*

Easy biographies which give the action and color of early America.

Instant Readers. Holt, Rinehart and Winston. 1971.

Level I	Level II	Level III
Brown Bear, Brown Bear, What Do You See?	*Ten Little Squirrels*	*Whistle, Mary Whistle*
When It Rains, It Rains	*My Days are Made of Butterflies*	*Old Mother Middle-Muddle*
Monday, Monday, I Like Monday	*The Happy Hippopotami*	*City Sons*
The Haunted House	*"Tricks or Treats?"*	*Old Devil Wind*
Up and Down the Escalator	*Welcome Home, Henry*	*A Spooky Story*
The Wizard	*The Maestro Plays*	*King of the Mountain*
Silly Goose and the Holidays	*I Paint the Joy of a Flower*	*The Little Disaster*
A Ghost Story	*The Eagle Has Landed*	*I'm Going to Build a Supermarket One of These Days*
Fire! Fire!	*Turning of the Year*	*Tatty Mae and Catty Mae*

I Went to the Market	*What to Say and When to Say It*	*The Longest Journey in the World*

Johnson, Margaret S. *Silver Dawn.* Morrow, 1958.

Reading Level: grade 4
Interest Level: grades 4-8

A story of a show horse. A similar title is: *Gavin, A Scottish Deer Hound.* These are good for reading aloud.

Judson, Clara I. *Green Ginger Jar.* Houghton, 1949.

Reading Level: grades 5-6
Interest Level: grades 7-8

Chinese Life in Chicago is pictured in this mystery tale. Junior high school boys and girls should enjoy this.

Junior Science Books. Garrard, 1960-1965.

Reading Level: grade 3
Interest Level: grades 2-8

Collins	*Turtles*
Crosby	*Beavers*
Crosby	*Stars*
Feravolo	*Electricity*
Feravolo	*Flying*
Feravolo	*Light*
Feravolo	*Magnets*
Larrick	*Rain, Hail, Sleet, and Snow*
Lauber	*Penguins*
Lauber	*Volcanoes*
Lemmon	*Big Cats*
Sheldon	*Elephants*

Easy, accurate information on various aspects of natural science. There are several other suitable titles in this series.

Kaler, James O. *Toby Tyler.* World, 1947.

Reading Level: grade 5
Interest Level: grades 7-8

Toby runs away to join the circus but finds that home is best after all. Intermediate grade children would enjoy having this read to them.

Larom, Henry V. Miller. *Bronco Charlie.* McGraw, 1951.

Reading Level: grades 3-4
Interest Level: grades 5-6

Eleven-year-old Charlie's dream comes true when he unexpectedly rides for the pony express. A true incident.

Lenski, Lois. *Cowboy Small.* Walck, 1949.

Reading Level: grades 1-2
Interest Level: grades 1-4

A very simple picture story about Cowboy Small and his horse, Cactus.

Litchfield, Ada B. *I Can, Can You.* Steck-Vaughn, 1971.

Reader Level: grade 1
Interest Level: grade 2

Delightfully nonsensical.

Leonard, Rhoda, *Wildlife Adventure Series.* Harr Wagner, 1964-1966.

	Reading Level	*Interest Level*
Gatie the Alligator	Gr. 4	Grs. 2-8
Sleeky the Otter	4	2-8
Skipper the Dolphin	4	3-8

Lewis, Thomas. *Hill of Fire.* Harper, 1971.

Reading Level: grade 1
Interest Level: grade 2-3

The story contains human interest and in addition includes information about the Mexican Vulcano, Paricutin.

Tawny the Mountain Lion	Gr. 4	Grs. 3-8
Bounder the Jackrabbit	5	4-8
Thor the Moose	5	4-8
Ruff the Wolf	5	4-8
Arctos the Grizzly	5	4-8

Fictionized life cycle and animal adventure stories which should appeal to boys.

McCall, Edith S. *Button Books.* Benefic, 1954-1959.

	Reading Level	*Interest Level*
Buttons at the Zoo	Preprimer	Preprimer-grade 2
Buttons See Things That Go	Preprimer	Preprimer-grade 2
Bucky Button	Preprimer	Preprimer-grade 2
Buttons and the Whirlybird	Primer	Primer-grade 3
Buttons Take a Boat Ride	Primer	Primer-grade 3
Buttons and the Pet Parade	Primer	Primer-grade 3
Buttons and Mr. Pete	Gr. 1	Grs. 1-4
Buttons at the Farm	1	1-4
Buttons and the Boy Scouts	2	2-5
Buttons Go Camping	2	2-5
Buttons and the Little League	3	3-6

Buttons and the Soap Box Derby 3 3-6

Family stories interesting to children through the primary grades. Bucky is 10 years old, other children younger. The father is a "blue collar" worker.

McClung, Robert. *Ruby Throat.* Morrow, 1950.

Reading Level: grades 3-4
Interest Level: grades 4-8

Life cycle of a hummingbird. *Stripe, Bufo,* and *Sphinx* by the same author are easy science stories also.

McGovern, Ann. *If You Sailed on the Mayflower.* Scholastic, 1970.

Reading Level: 1-2
Interest Level: 3-4

Appealing format, readable type, and authentic information make this an appealing historical reference.

Malone, Mary. *Annie Sullivan.* Putnam, 1971.

Reading Level: grade 3
Interest Level: grades 4-6

An authentic biography written to interest intermediate grade children with mature taste.

Mason, Miriam E. *Pony Called Lightning.* Macmillan, 1948.

Reading Level: grade 5
Interest Level: grades 5-8

An Indian pony outruns everything.

Montgomery, Elizabeth R. *Mystery of Edison Brown.* Scott, Foresman, 1960.

Reading Level: grade 3
Interest Level: grades 5-6

Adventure of two children who live on a lonely island, and the mystery they solve.

Obermeyer, M. B. *Six Robbens.* Scott, Foresman, 1950.

Reading Level: grade 3
Interest Level: grades 5-6

The Robbens family find and solve a mystery when remodeling an old schoolhouse into a home.

Radlauer, Edward. *Custom Cars.* Bowmar, 1968.

Reading Level: grades 3-4
Interest Level: grades 3-8 and up

Drag Racing
Drag Racing—Funny Cars
Dune Buggies

Dune Buggy Racing
Horses
Karting
Mighty Midgets
Motorcycles
Slot Car Racing
Surfing
Teen Fair

This sports series, copiously illustrated with photographs, in color, is especially designed for boys who are more interested in action than in reading.

Rambeau, John. *Jim Forest Readers.* Harr Wagner, 1959.

	Reading Level	*Interest Level*
Jim Forest and Ranger Don	Gr. 1	Grs. 1-4
Jim Forest and the Bandits	2^1	2-5
Jim Forest and the Mystery Hunter	2^2	2-6
Jim Forest and the Dead Man's Peak	3^1	3-7
Jim Forest and the Flood	3	3-8
Jim Forest and Lone Wolf Gulch	3	3-8

Exciting plots and much action in this series which contains many aspects of conservation.

Rambeau, John. *Morgan Bay Mysteries.* Harr Wagner, 1962.

	Reading Level	*Interest Level*
Mystery of Morgan Castle	Gr. 2	Grs. 3-8
Mystery of the Marble Angel	2	3-8
Mystery of the Midnight Visitor	3	4-8
Mystery of the Missing Marlin	3	4-8

Renick, Marion L. *Big Basketball Prize.* Scribner, 1963.

Reading Level: grades 2-3
Interest Level: grades 2-5

A popular basketball story. Other easier sports stories by this author and J. L. Renick are: *The Dooleys Play Ball, Touchdown for Doc, Wicky's Football Team, Pete's Home Run,* and *Tommy Carries the Ball.* Several of these are usable through grade 8.

Rey, Hans A. *Curious George.* Houghton, 1941.

Reading Level: grade 3
Interest Level: grades 1-6

This lively monkey appeals to all ages. It is followed by *Curious George Takes a Job, Curious George Rides a Bike, Curious George Gets a Medal,* and *Curious George Goes to the Hospital, Cecily G. and the Nine Monkeys* is also popular.

Rivers of the World Series. Garrard, 1961-1968.

Reading Level: grade 5
Interest Level: grades 4-7

Crosby	*The Rio Grande*
Epstein	*The Sacramento*
Latham	*The Chagres*
Latham	*The Columbia*
Weingarten	*The Nile*
White	*The St. Lawrence*

Easy material covering the history, geography, and life near and on the famous rivers.

Rounds, Glen. *Stolen Pony.* Holiday, Rev. ed., 1969.

Reading Level: grade 5
Interest Level: grades 6-8

A story of devotion between a dog and a horse. *Blind Colt* and *Ol' Paul the Mighty Logger* are easier to read. These could be read to younger children.

Sears, Paul M. *Barn Swallow.* Holiday, 1955.

Reading Level: grade 3
Interest Level: grades 3-7

The life cycle of a swallow. Another similar title by the same author: *Firefly.*

See and Read Beginning to Read Biographies. Putnam, 1964-1965.

Reading Level: grades 2-3
Interest Level: grades 2-5

An easy biography series which includes:

Martin	*Abraham Lincoln*
Martin	*John Fitzgerald Kennedy*
Olds	*Christopher Columbus*
Voight	*Nathan Hale*

Sports Series. Garrard, 1965-1968.

Reading Level: grade 4
Interest Level: grades 3-6

Epstein	*Game of Baseball*
Finlayson	*Stars of the Modern Olympics*
Newcombe	*Game of Football*
Reeder	*On the Mound*
Van Riper	*Game of Basketball*

Exciting, readable biographies of great sportsmen and histories of various games.

Steel, William O. *Daniel Boone's Echo.* Harcourt, 1957.

Reading Level: grades 3-4
Interest Level: grades 3-8

A hilarious tall tale. Other similar titles by this author are: *Andy Jackson's Water Well, Davy Crockett's Earthquake,* and *The No-Name Man of the Mountain.*

Stratton, Clarence. *When Washington Danced.* Scott, Foresman, 1938.

Reading Level: grades 4-5
Interest Level: grades 7-8

An easy tale of the American Revolution.

Toles, Elsie. *Secret of Lonesome Valley.* Harr Wagner, 1955.

Reading Level: grade 4
Interest Level: grades 4-8

A remedial reader full of adventure and excitement, woven around ranch life.

True Book Series. Children's Press, 1953-1965.

Reading Level: grades 1-3
Interest Level: grades 1-5

Some suggested titles in a long series are:

Ballard	*Reptiles*
Carlisle	*Automobiles*
Clark	*Dinosaurs*
Harmer	*Pioneers*
Leavitt	*Tools for Building*
Podendorf	*Space*
Podendorf	*Spiders*
Posell	*Deserts*

Easy, colorfully illustrated, and appealing.

Warner, Gertrude C. *Lighthouse Mystery.* Scott, Foresman, 1963.

Reading Level: grade 3
Interest Level: grades 5-6

This is a sequel to *Boxcar Children, Surprise Island, Yellow House Mystery, Mystery Ranch, Mike's Mystery, Blue Bay Mystery,* and *Woodshed Mystery.* An entertaining easily read adventure story.

Warner, Gertrude C. *1001 Nights.* Scott, Foresman, 1954.

Reading Level: grade 3
Interest Level: grades 5-6

An easy retelling of some of the Arabian Nights stories.

Wasserman, Selma. *Sailor Jack Series.* Benefic, 1960-1962.

	Reading Level	Interest Level
Sailor Jack	Preprimer	Preprimer-grade 2
Sailor Jack and Eddy	Preprimer	Preprimer-grade 2
Sailor Jack and Homer Pots	Preprimer	Preprimer-grade 2
Sailor Jack and Bluebell	Primer	Primer-grade 3
Sailor Jack and Bluebell's Dive	Primer	Primer-grade 3
Sailor Jack and the Jet Planes	Primer	Primer-grade 3
Sailor Jack and the Ball Game	Gr. 1	Grs. 1-4
Sailor Jack's New Friend	1	1-4
Sailor Jack and the Target Ship	2	2-5
Sailor Jack Goes North	2	3-6

Humor, adult characters, and fast-moving action with very easy vocabulary.

What Is It Series: Benefic, 1957-1965.

Easy, colorful descriptions of various aspects of science. Some of the titles are:

		Reading Level	Interest Level
Darby	*What Is a Simple Machine*	Gr. 1	Grs. 1-4
Darby	*What Is a Turtle*	1	1-4
Darby	*What Is the Earth*	2	2-5
Darby	*What Is a Chicken*	2	2-5
Darby	*What Is a Butterfly*	3	3-6
Darby	*What Is a Frog*	3	3-6
Kane	*What Is Space*	4	4-8
Munch	*What Is a Rocket*	4	4-8
Neal	*What Is an Insect*	4	4-8
Posin	*What Is a Dinosaur*	4	4-8
Posin	*What Is a Star*	4	4-8
Reuben	*What Is a Magnet*	4	4-8
Syrocki	*What Is Weather*	4	4-8
Wescott	*What Is a Rodent*	4	4-8
Wescott	*What Is a Reptile*	4	4-8

Wilder, Laura. *Farmer Boy.* Harper, 1953.

Reading Level: grade 5
Interest Level: grades 7-8

Autobiographical story of the frontier. Other suitable titles in the same series are: *Little House in the Big Woods, Little House on the Prairie*, and *On the Banks of Plum Creek.*

Wise, William. *The Spy and General Washington.* Dutton, 1965.

Reading Level: grades 4-5
Interest Level: grades 4-8

Based on a true historical incident, this exciting story tells of the adventures of an American spy for General Washington and how he helped turn the tide for the patriots.

World Explorer Series. Garrard, 1965-1969.

Reading Level: grade 4
Interest Level: grades 3-6

Blassingame	*Ponce de Leon*
de Leeuw	*Roald Amundsen*
Graves	*Henry Morton Stanley*
Knoop	*Vasco Nuñez de Balboa*

Exciting biographies of great explorers. Some other titles in this series at similar reading and interest levels are: *Fridtj of Nansen, Francisco Coronado, Marco Polo,* and *Amerigo Vespucci.*

Zim, Herbert S. *Elephants.* Morrow, 1946.

Reading Level: grade 2
Interest Level: grades 2-6

Physical characteristics and habits of elephants. Also *Great Whales, Owls,* and *Snakes. What's Inside of Engines?* is interesting to grades 7 and 8.

APPENDIX IV

Exploring Multi-Media Aids

While the two most important assets to the reading program are an amply stocked library and a capable teacher, areas of secondary importance, but well worth exploring, are the multi-media aids presently flooding the market. The following information is a point of departure in exploring investments that may serve to supplement your particular program.

Before discussing mechanical devices, it is well to review the crucial tools of the primary teacher. These include the development of independence in decoding, the building of sight words, and the matching of printed symbols with speech.

The overlapping goals are to develop fluency in oral reading as the child translates the author's words back to speech, and in silent reading as he responds to the author's words while they are translated through "central processing."

ACCELERATION DEVICES

Group-Control Reading Devices

In light of the goals for the elementary school child, devices for mechanically accelerating reading are obviously not wise investments. Students in this age group are still learning to apply flexible rates resulting from the difficulty of the material and the purpose for reading it. The following skeletal chart shows a comparison of rates that vary in accordance with the difficulty and purpose of the reading task:

Reference	*Difficulty*	*Purpose*	*Rate*
Telephone Book	Easy	To scan (search for a specific name)	500 wpm
Basal Reader	Instructional Level	To skim (rapid reading for main ideas)	180 wpm
Encyclopedia	Difficult	For detailed information	30 wpm

It is unprofitable to focus mechanically on speed before the child has learned to vary his speed with the difficulty of the content, and with his purpose for reading. It is much more rewarding to spend time in self-development programs, such as R/Q, $SQ3_R$, and EVOKER.

R/Q — as outlined in Chapter 7.

$SQ3_R$ — refers to survey, question, read, recall, (reread or review).[1]

EVOKER[2] — Explore. Silently read the *entire* selection.
— Vocabulary. Check unknown words.
— Oral Reading. Read aloud with expression.
— Key Ideas. Mark the beginning and end of each key idea.
— Evaluate. Evaluate each key word and sentence and the contribution they make to the main theme.
— Recapitulate. Read the entire selection slowly and completely, with insight and understanding.

Hopefully, after experimenting with all three of the above systems, the child will develop his uniquely effective approach to assigned reading. Certainly being an efficient reader is superior to being a speed reader with inflexible reading rates. Controlled readers and the Iowa and Harvard speed of reading films are more appropriately used at the secondary level rather than in the elementary level, except in the case of accelerated students.

Individual Pacer

However, after the child has met the criteria for an efficient reader, he may wish to experiment individually with a pacing device.

Helping the child learn how to pace his own reading so as to get the most information and enjoyment from it is one of the elementary school teacher's tasks. If the teacher has some advanced student whom she feels would be motivated by an individualized mechanical device, the Rateometer[3] at $39.95 is a simple, comparatively inexpensive pacer. It is easy for students to regulate, and there is very little that can go wrong with it. Model B with a range from 20 to 500 wpm would be appropriate for use in the elementary school classroom.

---

[1] Francis P. Robinson, *Effective Study* (New York: Harper & Row, 1946).

[2] From Walter Park, "On Scholarship: Advice to High School Students," *The Reading Teacher*, Nov. 1963, pp. 73-78.

[3] Audio-Visual Research, 531 South Plymouth Court, Chicago 5, Illinois.

However, even with the use of a simple bar descending the student's page, the transfer of the increased speed of reading to his usual daily reading rate will not occur unless an intermediate step is taken. Suppose a sixth-grade student increases his reading rate from 180 to 250 wpm on stories at the sixth-grade level; unless he then practices with his book *beside* the descending T-scope (which he can see peripherally), it is likely that he will regress to his original rate of 180 wpm. By taking the intermediate step, the student becomes more accustomed to the rate without being *directly* pushed by the descending bar.

Tachistoscopic Devices

Many claims are made for the value of tachistoscopic training. However, even the inexpensive tachistoscopic equipment can be defended on three grounds only:

The device:

- catches the attention of the students
- causes them to attend to the flashed stimulus in which extraneous detractors are minimal
- results in students responding favorably to a change of pace

Other claims popularly advanced, such as increased span of recognition and speed of comprehension, are not substantiated by research design tight enough to control important variables, such as the teacher, time and money spent, and the Hawthorne effect.

Exercises to increase the span of digit recognition have no carry-over into text or literary reading. Nevertheless, if a teacher has a group of hyperactive boys interested in numbers, she could include digit recognition for its motivational value. Indeed, she might hope that the *fun* of recognizing numbers rapidly would spill over into the area of recognizing phrases quickly and accurately. A measure which helps in the transfer of a rapid-response skill is to use the same words and phrases in duplicated material and determine the rate at which they are located by the students. An additional step is to have the students read a passage silently before tachistoscopic practice, and again after this practice. Compare the difference in reading rates. For the student who gains only slightly or not at all, the device is ineffective and other techniques should be substituted.

Hand-Made Tachistoscope

A simple tachistoscopic device can be made by cutting out from an index card a narrow aperture the size of the longest typed phrase to be used. Staple another index card on the back. Cut a long strip of tagboard wide enough to contain typed phrases, but narrow enough to slide between the two stapled index cards, as illustrated. (See Figure IV-1.) Select phrases from the book which the child is reading. Customarily, this device is used by the teacher and student working together, but it may be used by two students.

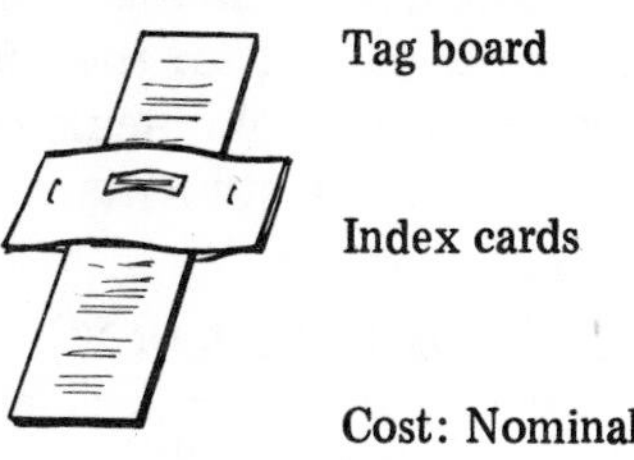

Figure IV-1

Tach-o-Flasher

The least complicated triggered tachistoscope is a commercially made Tach-o-flasher[4] (Figure IV-2). This device is placed in front of a filmstrip projector. The speed of this simple instrument is 1/40th of a second, if triggered rapidly by hand. The shutter can be adjusted to remain open for students to check the correctness of their responses. This device is especially appropriate for children who need practice in instant recognition of high-frequency words, since the filmstrips that are commercially made utilize these words individually and in phrases.

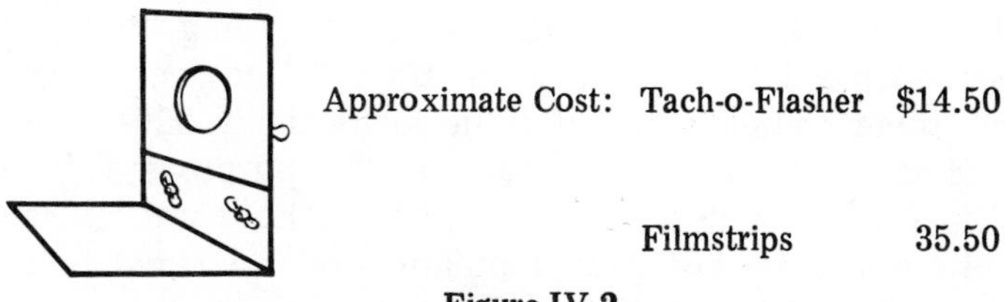

Approximate Cost: Tach-o-Flasher $14.50
Filmstrips 35.50

Figure IV-2

In general, it can be stated that expensive tachistoscopic devices are an inappropriate expenditure for most elementary schools. The average adult reader takes 1/6th of a second

[4]Instant Word Phrases, Learning Through Seeing, Inc., Sunland, California 91040.

between fixations and a 252-millisecond fixation in which to integrate, match, and recall what he has seen.[5] Tachistoscopic devices set at 1/100th of a second place a heavier burden on the reader to speed up the usual 1/6th of a second scanning, while simultaneously allowing him more time in between fixations (to retrieve or reorganize and recall the briefly exposed stimuli). In this respect, the practice differs from the usual reading pattern and lacks enough identical elements to transfer easily into the reading act. Consequently, except for the focus of attention and the change of classroom pace, rapid tachistoscopic practice is of doubtful use for even secondary students.

AIDS TO FLUENCY

For the child who needs time to practice on his own, the following aids are helpful: the Language Master, Hoffman Gold Series,[6] and a Listening Post.

Language Master

A machine that is essentially an elementary school aid is the Language Master, priced at about $250. One set of cards costs approximately $35. It provides needed practice in seeing and hearing words simultaneously. It is of special value to children who are bilingual or who have speech or reading problems, because it permits them to hear good examples over and over again.

This unit consists of a rectangular machine through which cards are fed containing words and phrases. Such phrases as "Good Morning" and "How are you?" are run through the machine, and the child has the benefit of seeing the words at the same time that he hears them. He is, in fact, encouraged to repeat them immediately after he hears them. This machine, thus, is eminently well-suited for remedial purposes; it is not a good investment unless the needs of the school warrant it (the school has a large bilingual population or is located in a low socioeconomic area, for instance).

---

[5] Howard Walton, "Vision and Rapid Reading, "*American Journal of Optometry and Archives of the American Academy of Optometry*, Monograph 208 (Feb. 1967).

[6] Audio Graphic Supply, 788 North Waterman, San Bernardino, California 92410.

Hoffman Gold Series

The Hoffman Gold Series has high-interest, low-vocabulary albums, and while the Mark IV is an expensive machine costing approximately $380, it has low maintenance. Album sets contain four flat, durable filmstrips and two records which can be clicked into the machine. The content of the albums is informative, appealing, and instructive. Considering the number of teacher hours it would take to prepare similar tapes to be used with existing filmstrips, the unit would seem to be a wise investment. By having several rooms share this equipment, the cost seems justified.

Listening Post

In an earlier chapter, reference was made to a Listening Post. An area equipped with this audio aid fills a definite need in the progressive classroom, but many teachers feel that the cost is prohibitive. However, with some ingenuity and simple directions, it is possible to build a four-station unit at minimal cost. This unit can be used with a standard tape recorder or record player. Sketches and an itemized list of approximate costs are included in Figure IV-3.

LISTENING POST

Regular school table

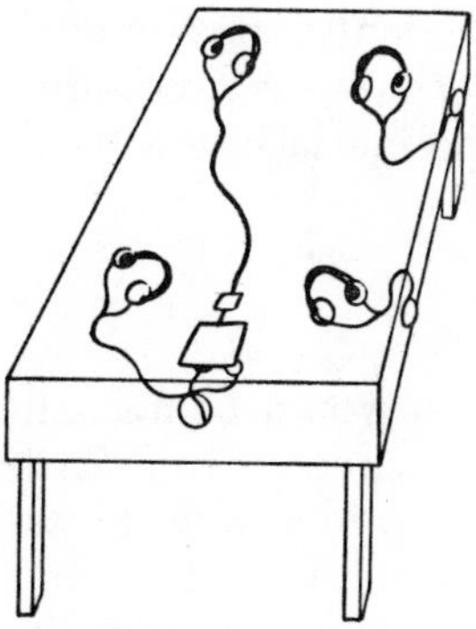

Amount	*Item*	*Approx. Cost*
2	¼" phone plugs @ .50	1.00
5	¼" standard phone jacks @ .40	2.00
1 roll	hookup wire	.50
4	headphones 8 (ohm) @ 2.50	10.00
1	10 (ohm) SL ½-watt resistor	.20
		13.70

Schemata

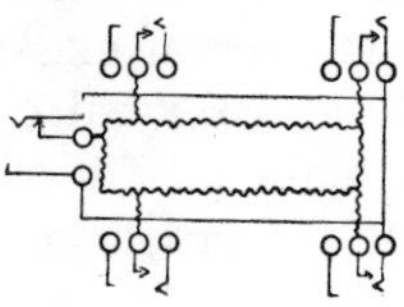

Figure IV-3

At times, the Listening Post can also be combined with a filmstrip projector. A small lightweight projector, easy for children to manage, is produced by the Herbert M. Elkins Company, Tujunga, California, at a cost of $44.95. The 3-inch lens is just right for projecting on a regular study table.

One of the most popular uses of the Listening Post is in coordinating tapes with reading activities. The newer sets (cassettes) are easier for students to handle than the traditional recorders, which require threading, splicing, and cautious rewinding. There are many excellent commercial tapes on the market—some of which allow for immediate student response. However, among the most effective recordings are those taped by members of the class and the teacher. These personalized recordings are relevant to the specific learning tasks and reading level of the class. These may cover a wide variety of activities—a few of which are:

1. Directions for other students to follow.
2. Poems and stories for others to follow in their own books.
3. Social Studies reports for others to listen to and follow.
4. Newspaper items for others to follow.
5. Captions synchronized with filmstrips.
6. Narrations to accompany silent films.
7. Original literary compositions read for the enjoyment of others.
8. Math problems to be solved as others follow each step.

The imaginative teacher will discover many other class activities suitable for taping by students to be shared at the Listening Post. Students are fascinated by this medium and enjoy using it daily. They appreciate the fact that in using tapes they are, in fact, directing their own learning. If a statement is puzzling to them, it can be played and replayed as many times as necessary. This, plus the concentration focused on the message, creates a productive climate for learning.

Projection Area

An ideal location for the projection area would be a small room off the central classroom. Since few schools can afford this, a table and several chairs may be set up in a quiet place away from main traffic patterns and direct sunlight. It is important that the projector itself be simple enough for students to operate with ease.

An inexpensive and practical screen for small groups can be constructed from a piece of cardboard by following the diagrams in Figure IV-4.

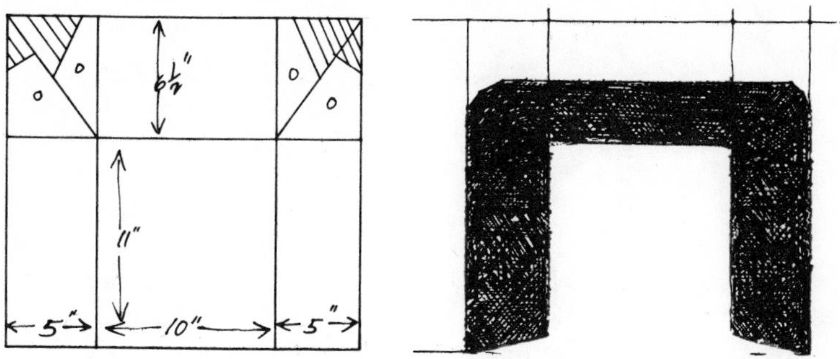

Figure IV-4

INDEX